Reviews of *Starting a Micro Business*

When my son started his teen business—which he eventually sold in a million dollar deal—he had little knowledge about how to structure it and handle the tax side. It was Carol Topp who helped him learn how to set up his business, keep records, and plan for future growth. Chris S.

Carol Topp's books not only helped me launch a successful micro business, but gave me the ability to run my business in an organized, professional manner. She has a simple, instructive, helpful writing style that is easy to understand and execute. The books have helped me accomplish one of the greatest goals I could ever achieve. Jade B., age 16

The book was amazing! With it I am making double minimum wage and I'm not even old enough to work at McDonald's or Kroger! The book has taught me that I don't have to be 15 to have a job! *Starting a Micro Business* has taught me how to manage my time and money wisely between my business, school, and other activities. Ethan E., age 14

Starting a Micro Business is the first business planning resource that I have seen that is geared specifically for teens who are thinking of starting a business. It is a great resource to help a teenager to learn about business and to ultimately start their own business. I strongly recommend this book and its very practical, doable approach to any aspiring young entrepreneur. I think it is provides teens a great first step into the entrepreneurial world. Michael P. Licata, Ph.D, Accounting Professor, Villanova University

D1110745

Money and Taxes
in a Micro Business

by

Carol Topp, CPA

Ambassador Publishing
Cincinnati, Ohio

ISBN 978-0-9829245-3-2

Scripture taken from THE HOLY BIBLE, NEW INTERNATIONAL VERSION® Copyright © 1973, 1978, 1984 International Bible Society. Used by permission of Zondervan.

Cover Design: Dave Huff
Author Photo: Cathy Lyons

Disclaimer and Limitation of Liability
This book is designed to provide accurate and authoritative information about the subject matter covered. The author is not rendering legal, accounting, or other professional advice.

The fact that a company, organization, or website is mentioned does not mean that the author endorses the information or services provided. The resources mentioned in this book should be evaluated by the reader. Readers should also be aware that organizations and web sites mentioned may have been changed or ceased operations since the publication of this book.

Any tax advice contained in this book was not intended or written to be used, and cannot be used, by any taxpayer for the purpose of avoiding penalties that may be imposed under the Internal Revenue Code or applicable state or local tax law provisions. Furthermore, this book was not intended or written to support the promotion or marketing of any of the transactions or matters it may address.

This book is dedicated

to my family: Dave, Emily, and Sarah;

to my teenage micro business clients,

Phillip, Lucas, Emily, Matthew, Lauren, Meghan,

and many more,

to Amanda Bennett,

who encouraged me from the start,

to all the homeschool families

who told me they wanted this book,

and to the Lord.

Table of Contents

What to Do If Cash Flow Is Negative
Learn From Your Mistakes

Unemployment Taxes
Workers' Compensation
Employer Forms

How Sales Tax Works
State Requirements
Consult with a Local CPA
Obtain a Vendor's License
Out-of-State Sales
Internet Based Sales
Paying the Sales Tax

Alternatives to Hiring Employees
Two Categories of Workers
Worker Classification: A Critical Issue
How to Determine Worker Status
Can't Decide? Let the IRS Help
Forms for Independent Contractors

What a CPA Can Do For You?
How Much Do CPAs Charge?
Questions to Ask an Accountant
CPAs Speak IRS-ese

Introduction
What's Different About
This Book?

I wrote this book because I knew that teenagers needed it. As a mother of two teenagers, I have met plenty of students that wanted to make some money, but didn't know how to get started. I also met a few ambitious students who did make serious money by creating websites and mowing grass, but they needed help with business issues. I started searching for books to help these teenagers.

I didn't like what I found.

There are plenty of books for kids who want to start a business like a lemonade stand. They are geared toward children who are just playing at running a business. They are usually cute books that explain the difference between quarters and dollars and how a bank is a safe place to put your money.

That's necessary information for children, but teenagers need more.

There are plenty of books for people wanting to be entrepreneurs. They are usually geared toward young adults just out of college. The assumption in these books is that the reader can get a bank loan (most teenagers cannot) or that the reader has plenty of time to devote to starting a business.

These books do not consider that a teenager needs to do homework, eat, sleep and still have a social life.

Finally, I ran across a few (but very few) books for teenage entrepreneurs. Some were books written for adults that were repackaged for teenagers by substituting a few words here and there. They were full of unrealistic ideas. I found one book that recommended a teenager open a restaurant! As if a teenager has the time (or money) to run a restaurant! Other books were full of inspiring stories about teen entrepreneurs, but they left me feeling intimidated because the teenagers featured were so very successful.

Their stories seemed beyond the grasp of a normal American teenager.

Some of the information in these books was useful, but they were inadequate in many areas. Few covered business plans. Even fewer discussed taxes in an intelligent and helpful way. There were rarely examples of how to keep good records and very few real life examples.

So I wrote this book because I knew that teenagers needed it.

This book is geared toward teenagers and their lives. There are no unrealistic expectations of opening a restaurant. There are ideas of businesses that real teenagers have started and run successfully. I provide a lot of examples of teenagers I know personally. I walk you through some very important topics such as making a plan and avoiding debt.

That's how this book is different!

This book is very practical. If you want inspiration, it's here in small bites, but primarily this book will be helpful and useful to you. Think of it as getting a CPA's advice for under $20.00!

Chapter One
How Successful Are You?
Your Income Statement

Is your micro business successful? Your answer depends on how you measure success. A micro business owner can be considered very successful even if he does not make any profit because he values what he has learned, perhaps more than the amount of money made. Another micro business owner is successful if he reaches a financial goal. Sometimes success is measured by the number of customers served and not in having huge profits.

In every business, micro, small or large, the owner needs to be able to measure the financial success of his or her business. An owner should know if his business is making a profit or just breaking even. He also needs to be able to see where he is spending his money, specifically, his various expenses. The tools a micro business owner uses to measure success are called the financial statements.

There are only a few financial statements that a business owner needs to review, but they can tell a lot about the health of a venture. There are several types of financial statements, but for a micro business, only two statements are essential: the income statement and the cash flow statement.

Some people call an income statement a profit and loss statement, or P&L for short. If you want to sound impressive, start talking about your P&L being "healthy." It is a technical way to say that you are making a profit. This chapter will explain the income statement. The next chapter explains the cash flow statement, how it works and why it is important in your business.

Income Statement

An income statement is a very popular financial statement for business owners because it is easy to understand. An income statement is a listing of business income and expenses over a period of time. Think of it like a video of people coming in and out of a bank. Some people deposit money into the bank. They would be similar to you earning money in your micro business and depositing the cash. Other people are withdrawing money from the bank, just as you will spend money on expenses for your business such as website hosting or office supplies.

The video runs for a specific amount of time—a day, month, or year—and the bank president can add up the deposits and subtract the withdrawals over any period of time he wishes. In the same way, an income statement for your micro business covers a period of time, usually a month or a year.

Parts of an Income Statement

Income

An income statement has two main parts: first, a list of all your income, and second, a list of all your expenses. The "bottom line" is at the bottom and shows the difference between income and expenses, hopefully as a profit and not a loss.

The categories of income are:

- Sales income. This is the money you bring in from selling your product or service. For a micro business, this is usually the largest category. Sometimes it is the only category of income.

- Sale of assets. This category is for income from selling off unneeded business equipment like an old computer. This is rarely used by micro businesses because they do not usually own a lot of equipment.

- Interest earned on a business savings account. Many micro owners keep their surplus in their checking accounts that do not pay interest and, therefore, rarely show business interest income. But if you are successful, you may set aside some of the profit in a savings account and earn interest.

Cost of Goods Sold

Sometimes the Cost of Goods Sold (COGS) is included with the other expenses, but accountants are taught to show it separately. Additionally, the sole proprietorship tax return, Schedule C, shows the COGS separately.

COGS is the value you paid for the products you sold. For example, if you sold 100 books that cost you $3 each, your COGS is $300. COGS is calculated from the value of inventory at the beginning and end of a period. Calculating your inventory value is very important. If you do not value your inventory correctly it makes your COGS number incorrect and that makes your bottom line—your profit—incorrect. Since COGS goes on your tax return, you could be repeating errors there.

COGS is calculated like this:

> Beginning Inventory
> + Purchases made throughout the year
> - Ending Inventory
> Cost of Goods Sold

The beginning inventory and ending inventory values are in dollars and come from counting your inventory and multiplying by the value of each item.

> **Example:** Lee sells books. She has no books at the start of her year. That means her beginning inventory is zero. She buys 100 books for $2.50 each from a printer (totaling $250 in purchases). At the end of the year she counts her books. She has 14 left.
>
> Here is how Lee calculates her COGS:

Lee's COGS

Beginning Inventory	$0.00
Plus Purchases	$250.00
Less Ending Inventory	-$35.00
(14 books at $2.50 each)	
COGS	$215.00

Lee's is a pretty simple example because she sells only one book title. Calculating the Cost of Goods Sold would be more complex if Lee sold several titles, each with a different cost to her. The record keeping can become quite complicated. Small business accounting software such as QuickBooks is extremely helpful for tracking inventory and the software calculates COGS no matter how many items you sell. If you have more than one product, you should seriously consider buying software. My book, *Running a Micro Business,* has a chapter devoted to using software to calculate COGS.

Expenses

The second portion of an income statement lists the expenses. Your expenses will depend on your type of business. There can be a lot of variety in your business expenses, so I recommend micro business owners use the categories listed on the Internal Revenue Service (IRS) tax forms, especially Schedule C Business Income and Loss. You can see a Schedule C in Chapter Five on federal taxes or at the IRS website, **www.IRS.gov**. Some common categories of expenses are:

- Advertising
- Car or truck expenses
- Contract Labor

- Insurance
- Legal and professional fees
- Office expenses
- Rent or lease equipment
- Supplies
- Taxes and Licenses
- Travel, meals and entertainment
- Utilities (cell phone and internet charges)
- Cost of Goods Sold (As mentioned earlier, some small businesses include COGS in the expenses, while others list it separately.)

Your micro business may only use one or two of these categories; it would be rare for a micro business to use all of them. Choose which categories best fit your business and group your expenses into those major categories. I discuss recording expenses using a simple bookkeeping system in my book *Running a Micro Business* available at **MicroBusinessForTeens.com.**

Bottom line
An income statement has a bottom line called *net income* (or sometimes, unfortunately, *net loss*). Net income is total income minus total expenses. If your business made more income than expenses, you have positive net income, called profit. If you spent more than you made, you have negative net income or a loss for the period.

Sample Income Statement

Here's an example of an income statement for one month of a micro business that offers piano lessons:

As you can see, this micro business has a pretty simple

Income Statement for March 2010	
Income	
Piano lessons	$82.50
Interest Income	$1.50
Total Income	$84.00
Expenses	
Advertising: fliers	$5.75
Supplies: Sheet Music	$9.50
Total Expenses	$15.25
Net Income	$68.75

income statement with only a few types of income and expenses. The owner brought in $84.00 in March, but shows a profit of only $68.75 after a few expenses. Notice how this micro business had only two categories for all of its expenses: Advertising and Supplies. This business has no Cost of Goods Sold because it is a service-based business with no products to sell.

Example with Cost of Goods Sold (COGS)
If your micro business sells products, you will need to know the Cost of Goods Sold and show it on your Income Statement.

Example: Julie owns a craft business and has only three expenses: her website, booth rental fees at craft shows and sales tax. As you can see, she sells over $1500 in crafts, but her profit is only $532, because her cost of goods sold is significant at $785.

Income Statement for 2010	
Income	
Sales	$1,575.00
Cost of Goods Sold	-$785.00
Gross Margin	$790.00
Expenses	
Advertising (website)	$60.00
Booth rental	$120.00
Sales tax	$78.00
Total Expenses	$258.00
Net Income	$532.00

How to Prepare an Income Statement

If you have been keeping good records as shown in *Running a Micro Business*, then preparing an income statement is very easy. Add up all of your income for a period of time (monthly is recommended) and then add up your expenses by category. List the income at the top of a page and the expenses by category below. Then calculate the bottom line of net income or loss by subtracting the expenses from the income. Use the example above as a guideline.

If you are using a spreadsheet program to keep records, it's very easy to summarize the information into an income statement. Using accounting software like QuickBooks makes it even easier to prepare an income statement. A few clicks and the software prepares the report for you. All you do is pick the time period (last week, last month, this year so far, etc.).

How often to prepare an income statement
Many business owners like to see an income statement for every month. Monthly reports are a good idea because if you wait too long to prepare an income statement, you lose track of the success of your business. You may not know if you are making money or losing it.

In addition to monthly income statements, micro business owners should add up the monthly totals every quarter (i.e. every three months, such as January through March, April through June, etc.). These quarterly reports can show your micro business's success over a longer period of time. Finally, a business owner should prepare an income statement at the end of the year. This is helpful for tax preparation and as a summary of the success after an entire year.

Balance Sheet

Another financial statement that can be helpful to a micro business owner is called the balance sheet. If the income statement is a video over time, then the balance sheet is a snapshot. A balance sheet lists assets (what you *own*) and your liabilities (what you *owe*) at a point in time, a single date. It could change tomorrow as you pay off a bill (a liability that you owed) or make a sale and add the cash to your bank account (an asset that you own).

Balance sheets are very useful for larger businesses, but are used less frequently in a micro business. In order to understand why, I need to explain briefly what a balance sheet looks like. A balance sheet has three parts: Assets, Liabilities, and Owner's Equity.

Assets

Assets are what you **own**, typically cash and equipment used in your business. For many teenage micro business owners, their assets might be the cash in their business bank accounts. They may also have bought some inventory or equipment to use in their business. Those are also assets. Sometimes you perform a job, but don't get paid at the time. Someone still owes you money. Since you have a right to that money, it is considered an asset. Earned, but unpaid, income is called accounts receivable, meaning that you are supposed to receive money from someone.

Typical Assets (what you own):
- Cash such as paper money, checking accounts, savings accounts and even the balance in a PayPal or eBay account.
- Equipment such as a computer, cell phone, sewing

machine or lawn mower that you purchased for the business.

- Inventory. The value of your products to sell at their cost (purchase price), not the retail price at which you hope to sell them.
- Accounts Receivable is money you expect to receive from your customers for work you already performed.

Liabilities

Liabilities are what you *owe* others. As a micro owner, you rarely owe anyone, but it can happen. Typical liabilities for a micro business include accounts payable and loans. Accounts payable are payments that you owe someone for work they have done for your business. Examples include hiring an independent contractor to do web design. Loans are any amount of money you borrowed to start your micro business and still owe the lender. Usually, micro businesses start with no debt or pay back their initial start-up loans very quickly.

Owner's Equity

The final portion of the balance sheet is where the balancing takes place. It's called owner's equity or net worth. It is the sum of three things:

- Your original investment into the business such as your start up expenses or the money from your savings account that you used to start the business.
- The sum of all your earnings (profit) since the beginning of your business (called retained earnings). This is called accumulated earnings.
- Your net earnings for the year so far minus whatever you have taken out for personal use. When you take money out of your business it is called an own-

er's draw. These earnings left the business and were used by you for personal use. The balance sheet shows owner's draws under owner's equity rather than as an expense of the business on the income statement.

Example: Julie's craft business has been in operation for three years. Initially, she borrowed $150 from her parents to start the business. She has made a profit each year and her accumulated earnings for the past three years add up to $418. This year she has a profit of $532 so far. Finally, Julie has withdrawn $400 from her business for her personal use this year. Her owner's equity would be displayed as this:

Owner's Equity	
Initial Investment	$150.00
Accumulated Earnings	$418.00
Net Earnings This Year	$532.00
Less: Owner's Draw	-$400.00
Owner's Equity	$700.00

The balance sheet is in balance when

Assets = Liabilities + Owner's Equity

Sample Balance Sheet

In this sample balance sheet, Julie lists cash, accounts receivable, and inventory as her only assets. She owes her parents a small loan of $150. Julie's balance sheet is balanced because assets of $850 equal the sum of liabilities ($150) and owner's equity ($700).

Balance Sheet for a Micro Business	
Assets	
Cash & Checking Accounts	$600.00
Accounts Receivable	$50.00
Inventory	$200.00
Total Assets	$850.00
Liabilities	
Accounts Payable	$0.00
Loans Payable	$150.00
Total Liabilities	$150.00
Owners Equity	$700.00
Total Liabilities and Owners Equity	$850.00

Who Needs a Balance Sheet?

I mentioned earlier that most micro businesses do not need to prepare a balance sheet very often, if at all. The best use of a balance sheet in a micro business is to see how much you own (your assets) and compare it to how much you owe (your liabilities). Your micro business is doing well if your assets are greater than your liabilities. You are headed for trouble if you owe more than you own.

In the sample above, the micro business owner is doing well because her assets are more than her liabilities. Julie can pay off all her liabilities (the loan of $150) with the money in her checking account.

Large businesses primarily use balance sheets when they desire to apply for a bank loan. Before loaning money, a wise banker will ask to see a balance sheet. They will look at the amount of debt a business already has and decide if the business is healthy enough to take on more debt. Most micro businesses do not have any debt. They use what they already have on hand, such as a computer, or build their business slowly as they make a profit. After all, most teenagers are in business to make money, not to be in debt!

In *Starting a Micro Business*, I discussed the dangers of starting a business with debt and offered many ways to start a business without any loans.

Other Financial Statements

My intention here is not to turn you into an accountant or bore you with numbers, but to simply expose you to a few necessary financial statements. You do not have to create a balance sheet yourself, especially if you use software like QuickBooks where reports like an income statement or balance sheet can be displayed in a second. But to make sure the statements are correct, you should have a little understanding of what those reports mean.

There are, of course, more financial statements that are generated in business such as return on investments, break even analysis, etc. I am not going to cover these statements in this book, but you can learn all about them from accounting and finance classes in college. For now, focus on the basics and learn more as your business grows.

You might consider taking a few accounting classes in college. You will learn a lot about running a business because accounting is the "language of business." Every business major takes at least two accounting classes in college. It is *that* important.

Did You Make a Profit?

Sometimes a micro business owner will have me prepare their tax return and have no idea if they made a profit or not until I tell them so. This may be because they are poor at record keeping, but perhaps they are confused about how to determine if they made a profit.

Simply put: Profit = Income – Expenses.

Profit is not the same as the balance in your checking account. You might think that you can look at the balance in your bank account to learn if you have made a profit, but that is probably not correct. To explain how to determine profit, here's an example of a teenage micro business.

Example: Emily runs a micro business teaching piano lessons. She had income last year of $850 from teaching five students. Her expenses were minimal, only $60 for buying piano books and rewards for her students. So Emily's net income is $790. Her income statement would look like this:

Emily's Piano Lesson Business Income Statement for Jan -Dec 2010	
Income	
Lessons	$850.00
Total Income	$850.00
Expenses	
Piano books	$55.00
Rewards	$5.00
Total Expenses	$60.00
Net Income (or Loss)	$790.00

Emily's balance sheet at the end of the year:

Emily's Piano Lesson Business Balance Sheet Dec 31, 2010	
Assets	
Checking Account	$42.00
Total Assets	$42.00
Liabilities	$0.00
Owner's Equity	$42.00
Liabilities & Owners Equity	$42.00

From Emily's income statement, she has a net income (profit) of $790 for the year, but only $42 in her checking account. Why the difference? Where did the money ($748 to be exact) go?

The profit Emily made was taken out of her business checking account and was spent (on iTunes, Starbucks, and movies to be exact). It's called an owner's draw. Taking money out of your business is a perfectly legitimate thing to do. That is the point of profit, after all—to spend it on your personal life. Owner's draws are not business expenses, they are withdrawals of the profit for personal use. They are shown on the balance sheet under owner's equity.

The details of Emily's owner's equity would look like this:

Owner's Equity	
Retained Earnings	$0.00
Net Income	$790.00
Owner's Draws	-$748.00
	$42.00

Emily had a net income of $790, but withdrew $748 for her personal use, leaving only $42.00 in the business as owner's equity.

But here's the big question: what gets reported to the Internal Revenue Service on a tax return? In other words, does Emily pay taxes on the $790 of net income or on the $42 left in her bank account?

She pays tax on her net income—her profit—which in this case is the $790. Let's hope Emily saved enough money to pay for those taxes! We'll cover paying taxes in another chapter.

Important Points

- An income statement is a very popular financial statement for business owners because it is easy to understand.
- An income statement (or P&L) is a listing of business income and expenses over a period of time.
- An income statement has a bottom line called *net income* (or sometimes, unfortunately, *net loss*). Net income is total income minus total expenses.
- If you have been keeping good records then preparing an income statement is very easy.
- Balance Sheets are not usually a necessary financial statement for a micro business. They are very useful for larger businesses.
- Profit is not the same as the balance in your checking account.

Chapter Two
Can You Stay in Business?
The Cash Flow Worksheet

If you want your micro business to stay in business, you need to understand cash flow. Positive cash flow is extremely important to the long-term success of your micro business. Positive cash flow is when you have more money flowing into your business than you have flowing out. It is a simple concept, but many micro businesses fail because the owner is not watching his or her cash flow.

> **Example:** Cindy loved to sell jewelry. She enjoyed setting up display tables with eye-catching table cloths, mirrors, and display stands. She also loved to thank her customers with gifts such as purses and cloth bags to store their jewelry. She saw all these expenses as important to her micro business. The problem was that buying purses, bags, and displays was causing more cash to flow out of her

business than into it! She had negative cash flow and soon had to quit her business. Instead, if she had predicted when she could buy more gifts or display items, she could have stayed in a business she loved.

Forecasting your cash flow is looking ahead to when cash will flow into your business and when it will flow out. Positive cash flow sustains a business. It is like fresh water into a lake. When the water flowing into a lake slows down or stops, the lake dies. When cash flow into your business slows or stops, your business dies.

A Cash Flow Worksheet

You should look at your cash flow on a regular basis, perhaps once a month. A cash flow worksheet is a useful tool. It contains a section titled *cash in* where you predict all the sources of cash coming into your business. A separate section, *cash out*, forecasts uses of your cash including money you may withdraw for your personal use.

It may be quite difficult to fill in some of the information on a cash flow worksheet. The worksheet asks you to make predictions on your sales and expenses. Expenses may be under your control, but sales can fluctuate quite a bit. It is still helpful to make an estimate. Use your past experience to predict sales for the future as best you can.

Cash Flow Worksheet

		Week (or Month) 1	Week (or Month) 2	Week (or Month) 3
	Cash In			
1	Cash you have right now			
2	Cash you can make from sales			
3	Customers who owe you money			
4	Cash from a loan			
5	**Total Cash In**			
6	**Cash Out**			
7	Supplies and Materials for Cost of Goods Sold			
8	Business Expenses (advertising, website fees, etc)			
9	Loan payments			
10	Owner's withdrawals			
11	**Total Cash Out**			
12	Cash Balance (Cash In- Cash Out)			

Sample Cash Flow Worksheet

Christy will be running a day camp for children in the summer. Christy has made some predictions on how long she will run the camp by doing a business plan and asking some potential customers about pricing. She has also predicted expenses for snacks and supplies for the camp. She decides she needs to invest some of her own money, $100, for the start up expenses of advertising and initial supplies. Christy's goal is to make a profit of $750 this summer for a class trip in late August. She must make a

$250 down payment by July 15. A cash flow worksheet will help Christy predict if she can go on the trip.

Cash Flow Worksheet for Christy's Kiddie Camp

For time period: June-August

	June	July	August
Cash In			
1 Cash you have right now	$100.00		
2 Cash you can make from sales	$500.00	$600.00	$300.00
3 Customers who owe you money	$0.00	$0.00	$0.00
4 Cash from a loan	$0.00	$0.00	$0.00
5 **Total Cash In**	$600.00	$600.00	$300.00
6 **Cash Out**			
7 Supplies and Materials for Cost of Goods Sold			
8 Business Expenses (advertising, website fees, etc)	$250.00	$150.00	$75.00
9 Loan payments	$0.00		$0.00
10 Owner's withdrawals		$250.00	$500.00
11 **Total Cash Out**	$250.00	$150.00	$75.00
12 Cash Balance (Cash In- Cash Out)	$350.00	$450.00	$225.00

Will Christy reach her goal of having $250 to make a down payment by July 15 and $500 by the end of the summer? She has positive cash flow each month, so that's a good start. It looks like she will have a positive cash balance at the end of June of $350, so that is enough to make the $250 down payment by July 15. She lists her withdrawal on line 10 as an owner's withdrawal. She should have enough cash at the end of August to pay for the trip in full with some money to spare.

How to Use a Cash Flow Worksheet

A cash flow worksheet is valuable because it forces you to think about the future and put a plan on paper. After you prepare a cash flow worksheet, ask yourself these questions:

- Does cash out exceed cash in? Why?
- Can I cut or delay some expenses?
- Are my loan payments too large for my cash in?
- Can I renegotiate my loan payments?
- How can I increase sales?
- What will it cost to increase sales?
- Can I afford to take money out of the business for myself?
- How much can I take out and still pay my expenses?
- Is my cash in low because I am waiting to be paid (a large accounts receivable)? What can I do to collect payments?

What to Do If Cash Flow Is Negative

Sometimes cash flow might be negative in a month. That does not mean automatic disaster for your micro business, because you may have some positive cash from prior months saved or know that the negative cash flow is just temporary.

You should be concerned if your cash flow is negative for several months in a row and shows no signs of getting better. If this occurs there are several things to do:

- Look at who owes you money. Remind these customers that they still owe you. When they pay, it will increase your cash in.
- Cut expenses to the bare bones.
- Renegotiate any loan payments. See if you can lower the payments and spread out the loan over more time.
- Do not take out more loans. Debt is not the way to increase cash flow. It is like trying to pour water into a leaky bucket. First, stop the leak!
- Consider offering a sale to increase cash in.
- Consider stopping all owner draws for a time. In other words, stop paying yourself for a while.

Learn From Your Mistakes

The cash flow worksheet is not much use if you do not learn from it. It is a great tool for you to measure how your business is doing and what you can afford to do in the future. Common mistakes micro business owners make include buying too much inventory, having a high cost of goods, or taking large withdrawals for themselves.

Have you taken on too much debt or ordered too much inventory?

> Terri made and sold Christmas crafts. She hoped to sell 1,000 mini Christmas trees at three craft shows in November and December. She spent a lot of time and money putting together 1,000 trees. Unfortunately, the craft shows were poorly attended and Terri sold only 250 trees. Now she has 750 mini Christmas trees to store in her basement until next

year. Her cash out was huge, but her cash in was weak. Next time, she will estimate more carefully how many crafts she can sell.

Did you spend too much on cost of goods sold?

Reggie makes delicious homemade fudge that is low-fat. He sells his fudge for $5.00 a box. He was buying his supplies from a local grocery store, but found that his cost of goods sold was $4.75 per box, giving him very little profit. He found a discount can-dy supply seller and bought ingredients in bulk low-ering his COGS to $1.95 per box. In order to buy in bulk, Reggie has to create a cash flow worksheet every month and save up cash to be sure he can afford to place an order.

Are you withdrawing too much money for yourself?

Lee was a successful author and her family grew dependent upon her income from selling books. She was withdrawing money every month from her busi-ness to pay for family expenses like groceries and entertainment. Unfortunately, she didn't create a cash flow worksheet and she did not have the cash to order more books from the printer. Instead, she had to order smaller quantities at a higher price and borrow money (with interest) to pay for the printing of more books.

Important Points

- Positive cash flow is extremely important to a micro business's long term success.

- Positive cash flow is when you have more money flowing into your business than you have flowing out.

- Use your past experience to predict sales for the future as best you can.

- A cash flow worksheet is valuable because it forces you to think about the future and put a plan on paper.

- You should be concerned if your cash flow is negative for several months in a row and shows no signs of getting better.

- The cash flow worksheet is not helpful if you do not learn from it. It is a great tool for you to measure how your business is doing and what you can afford to do in the future.

Chapter Three
Making More Profit

This chapter aims to help you make more profit, but first let's address why you want more profit. Naturally, you go into business to make money. Otherwise, you would be doing something else with your time. There is nothing wrong with making a profit, but you should consider your motivation for starting and running your micro business.

Motivation

In the first book in this series, *Starting a Micro Business*, I discussed all the reasons a teenager might start a micro business. They included to make money, to learn something, to test an idea, or to try out a potential career. Many micro business owners have a financial goal such as saving for an expensive item like a car or financing college.

Others hope that their micro businesses will be profitable enough to help them launch a bigger business.

Look back to your motivation and reasons for starting a business. Never lose sight of that reason when you become focused on making more money. Life is about more than making money; it is about learning, helping people, and stretching yourself to try new things.

Remember that a micro business can be successful if you have only one client or just break even financially. You can also measure success by how much you have learned or obstacles you have overcome.

If you have a financial goal and need to increase your profits, this chapter will get you started.

How to Make More Money

At some point in their lives, all micro business owners ask, "How can I make more profit from this business?" It's an age-old question, but it has a simple answer. There are only two ways to increase your profit from your micro business.

1. Increase Sales
2. Decrease Expenses

You can try one way at a time, or both at once for a bigger impact. Naturally, neither of these methods is easy, or you would already be doing them. I said they were simple, not easy!

Increase Sales

My earlier book, *Running a Micro Business* devoted an entire chapter to sales. Go back to that chapter and refresh your memory on how to increase sales. Add to that list a few more ideas to increase your sales.

- Advertise. Perhaps you need to look at your adverting and publicity. Maybe you need more customers, so work on getting out word about your business. Examine what has been successful in the past. Did emailing potential customers work well? Maybe it is time to send out another round of emails to remind people that your business can serve them. Persistence can pay off.

- Offer a sale. Everyone loves to buy things on sale. Maybe your customers are interested and just need to believe they are getting a great deal before they will buy from you. Be sure to tell them how much they are "saving" by purchasing during your sale period. Use phrases like "25% off" or "originally $19.95, now only $14.95."

- Hold a contest. Contests work well if you want to get out word about your business. Offer a free product or service for the winner of the contest.

- Develop a new sales promotion. Maybe you need to try a new selling angle, emphasize different benefits of your product, or change your sales presentation. Presenting the same product in a new way might get customers to see your product in a new way and buy from you.

Example: Catherine's babysitting service emphasizes her convenient after-school hours. During the summer Catherine offers to take children to neighborhood parks and swimming pools. Her advertising changes as the season changes.

- Try a new market. Brainstorm a few new markets that you have not tried before. Try to think of anyone who could use your services. If you mow grass for neighbors, branch out to small business owners and see if they need mowing or weeding.

- Take a survey and listen to your customers. What do your customers complain about? What are their needs? Ask them, "Is there anything else I can do for you?" You can survey them in person or by email. One fun tool to use is SurveyMonkey.com. You can create a 10 question survey for free and put it on your website. Ask what your customers want and then give it to them!

- Offer new services. If you serve your customers in one way, think of another way you could help them. If you babysit, offer to prepare dinner for the kids for an extra fee.

Example: Paul ran a lawn care service and listened to his clients complain about moles destroying their lawns. He decided to add a mole-trapping service and made more money from that new service than the original lawn care!

Decrease Expenses

Every dollar you can cut in expenses is a dollar of profit in your pocket, so cut those expenses. Consider carefully every expense, especially reoccurring expenses. What seems like "only" $20 a month can balloon to $144 a year.

In order to cut expenses, you must first know where you are spending your money. That starts with a foundation of good record keeping. In *Running a Micro Business,* I discuss the importance of recording all your expenses. Your bookkeeping really pays off when it comes time to cut costs (it also pays off at tax time!). If you have been recording all your expenses in a spreadsheet or software program, you should find it easy to create a report that shows your expenses summed up by category. Examine each category and look for expenses that can be reduced or eliminated. Consider nothing sacred (except paying your taxes!). Anything can be cut in order to make your business profitable.

Don't Cut Quality
Obviously, you want to avoid cutting the quality of your product. It will hurt sales if you find a new supplier that is cheaper, but sends you shoddy products. Your reputation is at stake, so sell the best quality you can afford to please your customers. Find cost-cutting measures in ways that do not disappoint your customers.

> **Example:** Patti ran a craft business and was paying $3.00 each for an important accessory on a purse she was selling. The purse was selling well at craft shows, but Patty wished to cut her expenses. She spent some time searching for a cheaper supplier and was amazed to find the accessory could be bought for $.50

each! That immediately increased her profit by $2.50 per purse!

Zero-Based Budgets

One technique for reducing expenses is to prepare a zero-based budget. A zero-based budget starts with $0 in every category of expense at the start of a year. You then justify every expense. This keeps the "fat" or overspending out of your budget.

This is a different method from the way most people prepare a budget. They usually look at last year's expenses and increase most categories by a small percentage, 2-4%, to account for normal inflation. This approach is quick and easy, but it does not cause you to seek out ways to reduce your expenses.

A zero-based budget forces you to ask, "How much *should* I be spending?" rather than, "What did I spend last year?"

> **Example:** Zach owns several websites and generates income from his ads on the sites and affiliate sales of software products. One of his major expenses is internet hosting fees. He spent $24.99 a month for hosting his various sites. That totaled $299.88 for the year.
>
> With a little hunting on the web, he discovered he could pay as little as $9.99 a month, but he was unsure that he would get the customer service and stability he needed. He didn't want to sacrifice quality for price. He went back to his web site host and found that they offered a discount if Zach paid three months at a time and a larger discount if he paid a year in advance. Zach saved almost $90 by paying for a year in advance.

Try doing what Zach did and shop around for a better deal occasionally. Ask if your current supplier will negotiate a lower price. Sometimes your current supplier will match a lower price that you found elsewhere just to keep your business.

Important Points

- Never lose sight of your initial reason for starting a micro business when you focus on making more money.
- Life is about more than making money; it is about learning, helping people, and stretching yourself to try new things.
- There are only two ways to increase your profit from your micro business: increase sales or decrease expenses.
- You can try many different methods to increase sales or decrease your expenses.

Chapter Four
Measuring Success:
Financial Ratios

In Chapters One and Two, I discussed how financial statements such as the income statement and the cash flow
worksheet can help you measure the financial success of
your business. In this chapter, you will learn about some
ratios you can calculate from those financial statements to
further analyze your business.

Financial ratios are used frequently in business to quickly
compare a business's performance against its history, its
future plans, or its competitors. There are literally dozens
of financial ratios that business analysts examine every
day, but for a micro business, only a few ratios are truly
helpful. In this chapter, we'll focus on only three ratios concerning sales, expenses, and your profit.

In order to calculate these ratios you will need to have financial statements prepared for several time periods, so you can make comparisons. Having at least a year of financial data is extremely helpful in calculating ratios.

Ratios From an Income Statement

There are several ratios that can be calculated from an income statement. They each measure the health of your micro business in different ways.

Cost of Goods Sold to Sales
This ratio tells you how much of every sale went into the product sold. It is desirable to keep this ratio as low as possible. The actual ratio can range from 5% to 95% depending on the type of business. For example, the grocery business has a Cost of Goods Sold to Sales ratio of 90% or more, meaning 90% of every sale made goes into buying the food products sold in the grocery store. A clothing retail store's ratio might range from 25-50%.

Frequently this ratio is compared to a previous period. If the ratio increases from 25% to 30%, the business owner may become concerned and will investigate why his costs are increasing.

It is calculated by using numbers from the income statement:

$$\frac{\text{Cost of Goods Sold}}{\text{Total Sales}} = \text{Cost of Goods Sold to Sales ratio}$$

Expenses to Sales

This ratio tells you how much of every dollar in sales goes to paying expenses. Like Cost of Goods Sold to Sales ratio, this ratio can range from 5%-95%, although 50% or less is typical. A business owner will be concerned if the ratio increases over time because it means his expenses are increasing (or his sales are decreasing).

$$\frac{\text{Total Expenses}}{\text{Total Sales}} = \text{Expenses to Sales ratio}$$

Net Income to Sales (sometimes called Return on Sales)

This ratio tells you how much of each dollar of sales you get to keep in profit. Naturally, a business owner wants high profits, but this ratio could be quite small, such as 1%-25%. A business owner likes to see this ratio improve over time, or at least not go down.

$$\frac{\text{Net Income (or Profit)}}{\text{Total Sales}} = \text{Profit to Sales ratio}$$

Gross Margin to Sales

This is a percentage that shows your markup on products sold before you have any other expenses.

$$\text{Gross Margin} = \frac{\text{Total Sales} - \text{Total COGS}}{\text{Total Sales}}$$

Example Using Financial Ratios

Lynn runs a craft business. Here is her income statement for a full year.

Income Statement for 2010	
Income	
Sales	$1,575.00
Cost of Goods Sold	-$785.00
Gross Margin	$790.00
Expenses	
Advertising (website)	$60.00
Booth rental	$120.00
Sales tax	$78.00
Total Expenses	$258.00
Net Income	$532.00

Lynn calculates a few helpful ratios from this income statement.

Cost of Goods Sold/Total Sales = $785/$1,575 = .50

Total Expenses/Total Sales = $258/$1,575 = .16

Net Income/Total Sales = $532/$1,575 = .34

(Total Sales-COGS)/Total Sales = $790/$1,575 = .50

These ratios tell Lynn that 50% of her sales go to pay the cost of the goods she sold, 6% of her sales go to pay expenses, and 34% is her profit. Another way to look at these ratios is in terms of the dollars of sales. For every dollar in sales, she spends $.50 on the cost of the goods she sold and $.16 on expenses such as advertising and booth rental fees; she gets to keep $.34 in profit.

How Ratios Help Your Micro Business

These ratios might be interesting, but how do they help Lynn run her business better? The ratios are most useful when you can compare them to something else, such as your past financial ratios, a competitor, or an industry standard.

Lynn's competitors are other craft sellers and they might not be willing to discuss their profits with a competitor, but Lynn could try to find financial information by searching her local library or the internet.

From **http://www.bizstats.com,** Lynn learns that retail clothing stores have a COGS/Sales ratio of .54 (or 54%) on average. Lynn compares this industry average to her ratio of .5 (or 50%), so she is close to an industry standard. On average, the Expenses to Sales ratio for the retail industry is 34%, almost double what Lynn has in expenses. Lynn keeps her expenses low by only selling at craft shows and not having to pay for a permanent store. Finally, a typical retail clothing store has a Net profit/Sales ratio of 13.4%, so Lynn feels happy that she is making 34% (or .34) of profit from her sales.

But Lynn knows that her micro business is very different from a retail clothing store (that's the closest industry standard she could find on the internet). The real value in the ratios comes from comparing Lynn's business to her past history.

Lynn compares her business ratios from 2010 to last year, 2009. Did she do better or worse in 2010? The ratios tells us that Lynn increased her Net Income to Sales ratio from .21 to .34, meaning that she used to keep only $.21 of every dollar in sales as profit for herself, but in 2010 she kept $.34 for every dollar in sales. She did better in 2010 than in 2009.

	2010	**2009**
$\dfrac{\text{Cost of Goods Sold}}{\text{Total Sales}}$	0.50	0.53
$\dfrac{\text{Total Expenses}}{\text{Total Sales}}$	0.16	0.26
$\dfrac{\text{Net Income}}{\text{Total Sales}}$	0.34	0.21

How did that happen? The ratios also tell us that Lynn has reduced her cost of goods sold from .53 to .50 and decreased her expenses to sales ratio from .26 to .16. So Lynn has done something to cut her Cost of Goods Sold and her expenses. This gives her more profit. These are all good trends that tell Lynn her business is improving.

Goal Setting With Ratios

Ratios can also be used as goals to achieve. Many businesses set a goal to have a Profit to Sales ratio that is better than last year. They track their progress throughout the year to see if they will achieve that goal. Having a goal to reach by improving a ratio can encourage business owners to cut expenses and have a healthier, more profitable business. Goals also motivate business owners to keep good records and to review financial reports—such as the income statement—on a regular basis to see how they are progressing.

Example: Robert runs a photography micro business. He wants to increase his Profit to Sales ratio from 40% to 50%.

Robert's Photography Business				
Goal: Increase Profit to Sales ratio from .40 to .50				
	Quarter 1	**Quarter 2**	**Quarter 3**	**Quarter 4**
Sales	$100.00	$100.00	$100.00	$100.00
Expenses	-$60.00	-$56.00	-$53.00	???
Profit	$40.00	$44.00	$47.00	???
Profit to Sales ratio	0.40	0.44	0.47	0.50

Robert's Profit to Sales ratio is improving every quarter all year long. He is getting close to his goal of .50 (or 50%). Robert must keep his expenses to $50 or less in the last quarter to meet his goal of a Profit to Sales ratio of.50 (or 50%).

I hope you can see how useful ratios can be, especially when used in comparisons to other businesses and to your own history. Make it a habit to create an income statement on a monthly or quarterly basis and calculate the ratios mentioned in this chapter. They will help you measure the financial success of your micro business.

Important Points

- Financial ratios are used to quickly compare a business's performance against its history, its future plans, or its competitors.
- Financial ratios are most helpful after you have been running your micro business for more than a year.
- The ratios are most useful when you can compare them to something else, such as a competitor or an industry standard.
- To achieve a particular ratio can also be a good goal for a business.
- Goals motivate business owners to keep good records and to review financial reports on a regular basis to see how they are progressing.
- Creating an income statement on a regular basis and calculating the ratios will help you measure the financial success of your micro business.

Chapter Five
Federal Taxes

I am frequently asked if a teenager owes taxes. The simple answer is "Yes, any American earning income, regardless of their age, owes tax." The difficult part to answer is how much does a teenager owe in taxes, because there are several types of taxes a teenager might pay and several exceptions to the tax laws for people under age eighteen.

In this chapter, I will focus on the taxes that apply to business income. There are other tax considerations that can affect teenagers such as investment income and earned income from a job, but for now we are only covering income from a business. For details on other tax situations, visit my website **TeensAndTaxes.com.** There you can order a copy of *Teens and Taxes: A Guide for Parents and Teenagers.*

Every sole proprietorship in America pays at least two types of taxes: federal income tax and self-employment tax. There are several other types of taxes, including employer taxes, sales tax, and state income tax, but federal income tax and self-employment tax are the two largest, so we'll begin there. State and employer taxes are covered in Chapter Seven and sales tax is covered in Chapter Eight.

Federal Income Tax for Business Owners

As a teenage micro business owner, you will report your net income from business (more commonly called profit) on a tax form called Schedule C Profit or Loss from Business and include the Schedule C with your Form 1040, the federal tax form for individuals. You should file your own tax return; do not report your business income on your parents' income tax return. You can still be claimed as a dependent on your parent's tax return (if you meet the dependency tests), so tell your parents not to worry that they will lose you as a dependent when you file your own tax return.

> **True Story:** When my daughter Emily started teaching piano lessons, she had to report her business income on Schedule C of her own tax return. My husband and I still listed Emily as our dependent on our own tax return. Naturally, since I'm a CPA, I prepared both tax returns. Your parents may want to get a CPA to help prepare the tax returns when you launch your micro business.

Schedule C (see on page 61 or at **www.IRS.gov/pub/irs-pdf/f1040sc.pdf**), is a listing of all your income and all your expenses from your micro business.

There is a simpler form called Schedule C-EZ. The Schedule C-EZ is only one page long and does not have you list all your expenses in detail; you just report your total expenses as one number. You can use the C-EZ form if:
- Your expenses are $5,000 or less
- You have no inventory
- You do not have a loss (a loss is when you spend more on the business than you made and therefore lose money)
- You have no employees or
- You have some other uncommon tax issues listed on the form C-EZ

In the following example, Tom Teenager made $7,550 in income from his micro business. He had no inventory of products to sell and no employees. He also had $525 in expenses, which Tom doesn't list in detail on his C-EZ, but he knows what they are, such as advertising, software, and internet fees.

His net income (profit) is $7,025 for the year. He will pay federal income tax and self-employment tax on that net income.

SCHEDULE C-EZ (Form 1040) Department of the Treasury Internal Revenue Service (99)	**Net Profit From Business** (Sole Proprietorship) ▶ Partnerships, joint ventures, etc., generally must file Form 1065 or 1065-B. ▶ Attach to Form 1040, 1040NR, or 1041. ▶ See instructions on page 2.	OMB No. 1545-0074 **20 10** Attachment Sequence No. 09A
Name of proprietor Tom Teenager		Social security number (SSN)

Part I   General Information

You May Use Schedule C-EZ Instead of Schedule C Only If You:	• Had business expenses of $5,000 or less. • Use the cash method of accounting. • Did not have an inventory at any time during the year. • Did not have a net loss from your business. • Had only one business as either a sole proprietor, qualified joint venture, or statutory employee.	**And You:**	• Had no employees during the year. • Are not required to file Form 4562, Depreciation and Amortization, for this business. See the instructions for Schedule C, line 13, to find out if you must file. • Do not deduct expenses for business use of your home. • Do not have prior year unallowed passive activity losses from this business.

A Principal business or profession, including product or service Web Design	B Enter business code (see page 2) ▶
C Business name. If no separate business name, leave blank.	D Enter your EIN (see page 2)
E Business address (including suite or room no.). Address not required if same as on page 1 of your tax return.	
City, town or post office, state, and ZIP code	

Part II   Figure Your Net Profit

1	**Gross receipts. Caution.** See the instructions for Schedule C, line 1, and check the box if: • This income was reported to you on Form W-2 and the "Statutory employee" box on that form was checked, or • You are a member of a qualified joint venture reporting only rental real estate income not subject to self-employment tax. } . . . ▶ ☐	1	7550
2	**Total expenses** (see page 2). If more than $5,000, you must use Schedule C	2	525
3	**Net profit.** Subtract line 2 from line 1. If less than zero, you **must** use Schedule C. Enter on both Form 1040, **line 12,** and **Schedule SE, line 2,** or on **Form 1040NR, line 13.** (If you checked the box on line 1, **do** not report the amount from line 3 on Schedule SE, line 2.) Estates and trusts, enter on Form 1041, line 3	3	7025

As you can see, Tom's tax return for his micro business is quite simple.

The Schedule C-EZ can be used by many micro businesses, but it is a good idea to become familiar with the longer Schedule C and the categories of expenses. I recommend you use these categories when recording your expenses to make tax preparation easier. Later in this chapter, I list many common business expenses that can be deducted on your income tax return.

SCHEDULE C (Form 1040)

Department of the Treasury
Internal Revenue Service (99)

Profit or Loss From Business
(Sole Proprietorship)

▶ Partnerships, joint ventures, etc., generally must file Form 1065 or 1065-B.
▶ Attach to Form 1040, 1040NR, or 1041.   ▶ See Instructions for Schedule C (Form 1040).

OMB No. 1545-0074

2010
Attachment
Sequence No. 09

Name of proprietor — Social security number (SSN)

A Principal business or profession, including product or service (see instructions) — B Enter code from pages C-9, 10, & 11 ▶

C Business name. If no separate business name, leave blank. — D Employer ID number (EIN), if any

E Business address (including suite or room no.) ▶
   City, town or post office, state, and ZIP code

F Accounting method: (1) ☐ Cash   (2) ☐ Accrual   (3) ☐ Other (specify) ▶

G Did you "materially participate" in the operation of this business during 2010? If "No," see instructions for limit on losses   ☐ Yes ☐ No

H If you started or acquired this business during 2010, check here . . . . ▶ ☐

Part I Income

1	Gross receipts or sales. Caution. See instructions and check the box if: • This income was reported to you on Form W-2 and the "Statutory employee" box on that form was checked, or • You are a member of a qualified joint venture reporting only rental real estate income not subject to self-employment tax. Also see instructions for limit on losses. ▶ ☐	1	
2	Returns and allowances	2	
3	Subtract line 2 from line 1	3	
4	Cost of goods sold (from line 42 on page 2)	4	
5	Gross profit. Subtract line 4 from line 3	5	
6	Other income, including federal and state gasoline or fuel tax credit or refund (see instructions)	6	
7	Gross income. Add lines 5 and 6 . . . . ▶	7	

Part II Expenses. Enter expenses for business use of your home only on line 30.

8	Advertising	8		18	Office expense	18
9	Car and truck expenses (see instructions) . .	9		19	Pension and profit-sharing plans .	19
10	Commissions and fees .	10		20	Rent or lease (see instructions):	
11	Contract labor (see instructions)	11		a	Vehicles, machinery, and equipment	20a
12	Depletion	12		b	Other business property . . .	20b
13	Depreciation and section 179 expense deduction (not included in Part III) (see instructions)	13		21	Repairs and maintenance . . .	21
				22	Supplies (not included in Part III) .	22
				23	Taxes and licenses	23
				24	Travel, meals, and entertainment:	
				a	Travel	24a
14	Employee benefit programs (other than on line 19) . .	14		b	Deductible meals and entertainment (see instructions) .	24b
15	Insurance (other than health)	15		25	Utilities	25
16	Interest:			26	Wages (less employment credits) .	26
a	Mortgage (paid to banks, etc.)	16a		27	Other expenses (from line 48 on page 2)	27
b	Other	16b				
17	Legal and professional services	17				
28	Total expenses before expenses for business use of home. Add lines 8 through 27 . . . . . ▶					28
29	Tentative profit or (loss). Subtract line 28 from line 7					29
30	Expenses for business use of your home. Attach Form 8829					30
31	Net profit or (loss). Subtract line 30 from line 29.					

When Does a Teenager Owe Income Tax?

The United States tax code is updated every year and the amount taxed can change from year to year. In 2012, a teenager with total earned income of $5,950 or more will owe federal income tax. The $5,950 amount is adjusted every year and is the same as the standard deduction allowed a single (unmarried) taxpayer.

This $5,950 (in 2012) includes your all your earned income from a job and your profit from your micro business. If you have earned income of less than $5,950, you will not owe any federal income tax. Great! But keep reading because you may owe other taxes such as self-employment tax or still need to file a return.

The US tax system charges you a percentage of your profit in income tax. These percentages are called tax brackets. The tax percentage rates (as of this writing) are
- 10% of your taxable income up to $8,700 (in 2012)
- 15% of your taxable income from $8,700 to $35,350

I tell you these rates (or brackets) to give you some idea of what percentage of your profit you will owe in federal income tax. The rates are subject to change (up or down!).

Notice the tax rates apply to your *taxable* income. Taxable income is your net income (or profit from your business) minus any deductions you get to take as allowed by the law. Every tax payer is allowed a standard deduction, even teenagers! The standard deduction for 2012 is $5,950 for a single (unmarried) taxpayer.

So to continue our example, Tom Teenager had a $7,025 profit from his business. He did not have any other earned income from a job. After he subtracts his standard deduction of $5,950 (something everyone gets to deduct, even teenagers), he has taxable income of $579.

Here is part of Tom's Form 1040 that shows his adjusted income ($7,025 all from his micro business minus some adjustments to equal $6,528), his standard deduction of $5,950, and his taxable income of $579. Tom owes federal income tax of $59 (line 44).

Tax and Credits	38	Amount from line 37 (adjusted gross income)	38	6,529
	39a	Check if: ☐You were born before January 2, 1947, ☐Blind **Total boxes** ☐Spouse was born before January 2, 1947, ☐Blind **checked** ▶ 39a		0
Standard Deduction for --	b	If your spouse itemizes on a separate return or you were a dual-status alien, check here .... ▶ 39b ☐		
● People who checked any box on line 39a, 39b or who can be claimed as a dependent, see instr.	40	**Itemized deductions** (from Schedule A) **or** your **standard deduction**	40	5,950
	41	Subtract line 40 from line 38	41	579
	42	**Exemptions.** Multiply $3,700 by the number on line 6d	42	0
	43	**Taxable income.** Subtract line 42 from line 41. If line 42 is more than line 41, enter -0-	43	579
	44	**Tax.** Enter additional tax if any from: a Form(s) 8814 ____0____ b Form 4972 ____0____		
●All others:	c	962 election ____0____	44	59

Notice on the form above that line 42 Exemptions is zero. This is because Tom is claimed as a dependent on his parents' tax return. Each person gets to claim one exemption for themselves and any dependents. Tom's parents will subtract $3,800 for Tom's exemption on their tax return. Tom does not subtract the $3,800 on his tax return, because his parents are using his exemption on their tax return.

Tom and his parents cannot both claim Tom's exemption. There is only one exemption to go around and usually parents take the exemption on their tax returns because their tax rates are higher and they can use every tax deduction and tax exemption they can get!

When Does a Teenager File a Tax Return?

Your micro business profit may be so small that you will not owe any federal income tax, but you may still need to prepare and send in a tax return. A tax return should be filed even if not required in at least three situations:

- Income tax was withheld from working on a job and you are due a refund of that money.
- Your micro business may owe self-employment tax (see below).
- Other specific situations involving investment income or loss may mean a teenager files a tax return. See my ebook, *Teens and Taxes: A Guide for Parents and Teens,* at **TeensandTaxes.com** for details.

Self-Employment Tax

In addition to federal income tax, there is another tax on the Form 1040 that affects teenage micro business owners. It is called self-employment tax (or just SE tax). SE tax is the same as Social Security and Medicare for self-employed people (micro business owners are self-employed because they do not have an employer—a boss).

The self-employment tax rate is approximately 15.3% of your micro's profit. If a student has net income (profit) of over $400 from a micro business, they will owe self-employment tax. The $400 threshold has not been adjusted in decades. Many teens who have micro businesses find that they may not owe federal income tax, but do owe self-employment tax. (at 15.3% of their profits!).

Additionally, there are no deductions or exemptions to the self-employment tax, unlike the federal income tax. This can come as a surprise to many teenagers and micro business owners.

Example: Tom Teenager had a net income (profit) of $7,025 in 2012 from his micro business. This was Tom's only income. As we saw above, he owes $59 in federal income tax. Tom will also owe $993 in self-employment tax (see Schedule SE, line 5 below). He owes more in self-employment tax than in federal income tax!

Section A---Short Schedule SE. Caution. Read above to see if you can use Short Schedule SE.			
1a	Net farm profit or (loss) from Schedule F, line 36, and farm partnerships, Schedule K-1 (Form 1065), box 14, code A	**1a**	0
1b	If you received social security retirement or disability benefits, enter the amount of Conservation Reserve Program payments included on Schedule F, line 6b, or listed on Schedule K-1 (Form 1065), box 20, code Y	**1b** (	0)
2	Net profit or (loss) from Schedule C, line 31 and Schedule K-1 (Form 1065), box 14, code A (other than farming). Ministers and members of religious orders, see page SE-1 for types of income to report on this line. See page SE-3 for other income to report	**2**	7,025
3	Combine lines 1a, 1b, and 2	**3**	7,025
4	**Net earnings from self-employment.** Multiply line 3 by 92.35% (.9235). If less than $400, **do not** file this schedule; you do not owe self-employment tax .... ▶	**4**	6,488
5	**Self-employment tax.** If the amount on line 4 is: • $106,800 or less, multiply line 4 by 15.3% (.153). Enter the result here and on **Form 1040, line 56.** • More than $106,800, multiply line 4 by 2.9% (.029). Then, add $13,243.20 to the result. Enter the total here and on **Form 1040, line 56.**	**5**	993
6	**Deduction for one-half of self-employment tax.** Multiply line 5 by 50% (.5). Enter the result here and on **Form 1040, line 27** **6**		497

Amazing? Yes it is! How can you reduce or eliminate paying the self-employment tax? There are four legal ways:

- Work as a household employee (discussed in Chapter Six).
- Work as a newspaper carrier. Paper carriers under age 18 do not pay self-employment tax.
- Work for your parents doing legitimate work in a business they own.
- Take every tax deduction you are legally entitled to take to reduce your net income (profit). This is where good record keeping pays off. The following section discusses legal tax deductions.

True Story: Beth started a craft business decorating flip flops with colorful cloth. She keeps her business very small because her goal is to learn a lot and have fun selling. She told me that her profit was always below the $400 threshold for paying self-employment tax. That's a tiny micro business! Beth's business may grow someday and then she will charge more so she has enough money to pay her self-employment tax.

Legitimate and Legal Tax Deductions

How can you reduce the taxes that you pay? The best legal way is to take every tax deduction you are allowed. Here are several tax deductions common to teenage micro business owners.

Mileage
The miles that you drive to a job or a client, to shop for business supplies, to the bank, or to consult with your ac-

countant are all business deductions. Keep track of the date, destination, and miles.

> **Tip:** To keep things simple, I record the miles on a calendar I carry in my purse. Sometimes I have to use Google Maps to calculate the mileage if I didn't check my car's odometer on the day of the trip. Some micro owners use their Blackberries or cell phones to record mileage. The IRS requirement is that mileage records be written, actual (not estimates or guesses), and kept "contemporaneously," meaning at the same time as the trip, not months later.

Business Use of Home
There is a business deduction called Business Use of the Home that allows a portion of your rent or mortgage payment, property tax, utilities, and insurance as tax deductions if a portion of the house is used *exclusively and regularly* for business. Only the owner of the home can take the deduction. Most teenagers do not own their homes; their parents are the owners, so the Business Use of the Home deduction cannot be claimed by the teenager. Your parents cannot claim the Business Use of the Home deduction for your business because the business is *yours*, not theirs. Sorry, but that's the law.

Meals
Meals with clients or for business purposes, such as at a conference, are deductible at 50% of their cost. Give your accountant the full cost of the meal and he or she will calculate the appropriate amount for tax purposes.

Clothes
If your work requires a costume or uniform, it is a legiti-

mate business deduction. Dry cleaning the special outfits is also deductible. Ordinary clothing that you can wear on the street is not a business expense, but is considered a personal expense and not tax deductible.

> **True Story:** A business owner purchased a suit to look more professional when he made some visits to potential clients. He didn't own a suit before he went into business. "Can I deduct it?" he asked me. No, sorry, the suit is not a business expense, but a personal expense because he can wear it on the street, for non business purposes. But I hope the suit got him the new client!

Office Supplies and Equipment

Office supplies, furniture, postage, and your computer are all business deductions. Also deduct any software you purchase to run your business.

Utilities

Most micro business owners do not have utilities (gas, electric, water, etc.) because they do not own a building for their business. But internet and cell phone expenses are utilities that are common in a micro business and can be a tax deduction. Internet and cell phone expenses should be split into business and personal use. The first phone line into a home is considered a personal expense and not deductible as a business expense.

> **Tip:** "How do I calculate the personal or business use of my cell phone," a client asked me. "Use a reasonable estimate," I told her. Any reasonable method such as the percent of time spent on the computer doing business versus pleasure can be used. Or if there are four people in the family, all us-

ing the computer but only one person uses the internet for business, it would be reasonable to consider 25% of the internet fees as business expense.

Advertising
Business cards, brochures, a website, and signs are all business tax deductions. If you put a sign on your car, then the cost of the sign on your car is a business expense, but not the car itself.

Education
Classes, conferences, trade journals, magazines, and books you read to enhance your knowledge of your business are business deductions.

> **True Story:** I subscribe to the Wall Street Journal. It greatly enhances my understanding of business, accounting, and taxes. The subscription cost is a business deduction. I also read *Simple Scrapbooking*, but it is for pleasure, not business, and is not a business deduction.

> **Tip:** The cost of this book is a business deduction!

Hired Help
Independent contractors and professionals that you hire for your business are legitimate expenses, even though they are not employees. Employee wages and associated payroll tax are business expenses.

> **True Story:** Phil hires independent contractors to do logo designs for his web hosting business. Lucas hired three friends as employees to help him cut grass in his lawn mowing business. Both these payments are business expenses.

Read more about hiring employees or independent contractors in Chapter Nine.

Taxes

There are several taxes a business might pay such as sales tax, payroll tax on employees, and property tax. These are all business expenses and allowed as tax deductions. Also, required licenses and government fees for a name registration or vendor's license are deductible. *Federal income tax and self-employment tax are not considered business expenses and not tax deductions*. State and local income taxes are also not business expenses.

Read more about sales tax in Chapter Eight and payroll and state income taxes in Chapter Seven.

It is important to know what expenses can be deducted on your tax return so that you pay less in taxes! If you have any questions about what expenses can be deducted on your tax return, ask your local CPA.

Important Points

- Federal income tax must be paid by micro business owners.
- Micro business profit is reported on Schedule C of the Form 1040.
- Self-employment tax is the same as Social Security and Medicare for self-employed people, including micro business owners.
- There are several business deductions that can lower what you pay in taxes.

Chapter Six
Who Are You? IRS Classifications of Teenage Workers

Are you a micro business owner, an independent contractor, or an employee? Sometimes it is not easy to tell. The same work, such as child care can be classified in three different ways depending on where you work, who you work for, and how you are paid. It can be confusing to many teenagers and their parents. Worker classification is important because it affects the taxes you pay—or do not have to pay—and that affects how much money stays in your pocket!

Employee or Independent Contractor?

When determining worker classification, we turn to the United States Internal Revenue Service (IRS) for definitions and guidance. The IRS classifies workers into two main categories:

- Employee: Someone performing services who is controlled by the employer in what is done and how it is done.

- Independent Contractor: Someone performing services where only the results of the work is controlled by the person hiring the worker; the means and method of accomplishing the work are not controlled.

Here are some examples. Can you tell the difference between the employee and the independent contractor?

> **Example:** Patrick, a web designer, submitted a job estimate for a website design and installation project that should take him about 12 hours. He is to receive a total of $180 from his customer, Betty's Beauty Spot, and will be paid $60 every week for the next three weeks. This is not considered payment by the hour. Even if he works more or less than 12 hours to complete the work, Patrick will receive $180. He also performs additional website design projects for other businesses that he obtained through advertisements. Patrick is an *independent contractor.*

> **Example:** Donna is a salesperson employed on a part-time basis by Blue Sail, a clothing boutique. She works 4 days a week and is on duty in Blue Sail's showroom on certain assigned days and times. She waits on customers, sets up clothing displays, and cleans the floors. Because of her experience, she requires only minimal assistance in run-

ning the cash register and setting up clothing displays. She is paid by the hour and is eligible for prizes and bonuses offered by Blue Sail. Donna is an *employee* of Blue Sail.

Is a micro business owner an employee or an independent contractor? Usually, they are independent contractors. The IRS tells us that people who have an independent trade, business, or profession in which they offer their services to the public, are generally not employees; they are independent contractors. I'll discuss independent contractors later in this chapter, but first you should be aware of a common exception to the rule.

Household Employee

I said the IRS classifies workers into two groups: employees and independent contractors, and that most micro business owners are independent contractors. But there is a common exception to that general rule: some micro business owners can run their own business, but still be considered employees. They are a special class of workers called household employees.

A household employee is a housekeeper, maid, baby sitter, gardener, or someone else who works in or around a private residence. Some examples from the IRS include:

- Babysitters
- Caretakers
- Cleaning people
- Domestic workers
- Drivers

- Health aides
- Housekeepers
- Maids
- Nannies
- Private nurses
- Yard workers

Household employees under the age of 18 are *not* considered self-employed micro business owners for tax purposes and so they do not pay self-employment tax.

Some micro businesses that teenagers can start are exempt (meaning free or excused) from paying self-employment tax. Avoiding self-employment tax can mean a lot more money in your pocket. Remember the example in Chapter Five when Tom Teenager had to pay $993 in self-employment taxes? The self-employment tax can get very expensive.

Several years ago a special category of workers was created called household employee. You can be classified as a household employee if:
- you are under age 18 at anytime during the year, *and*
- You are a student (meaning working is not your main occupation but being a student), *and*
- you work in or around a private residence as an employee (being an employee means that someone can tell you what to do).

All three things must be true.

So if you are under age 18 and want to avoid paying self-employment tax (and believe me, you want to cut taxes legally wherever you can), seriously consider a micro business that involves working in or around a private residence as a household employee. Lawn mowing and babysitting have long been great micro businesses for teenagers and now you know why—no self-employment taxes to pay!

> **Example:** Sarah goes to a neighbor's house and babysits their three children several times a month. In one month she made $75. She is a household employee. Sarah will not owe self-employment tax on her babysitting income. If she earns less than $5,950 (in 2012), she will not owe federal income tax, either. If Sarah decided to run a day care service during the summer from her home, she would not be a household employee, but rather a micro business owner. She will then owe self-employment tax (and, perhaps, federal income tax) on her profit.

Independent Contractor Status

Independent contractors are self-employed business owners. They are hired for a specific task or project (like plumbing or tax preparation), bring their own tools, work for several clients, and do not need training. Most micro business owners are independent contractors.

Examples of typical independent contractor jobs include:
- Website designers
- Computer repairmen
- Entertainers and musicians
- Editors and freelance writers
- Tutors

As I mentioned in Chapter Five on federal taxes, self-employed independent contractors must pay self-employment tax at approximately 15.3% of their profit. Self-employment tax is the same as Social Security and Medicare taxes. This is different from an employee who pays only *half* of their Social Security and Medicare taxes from their paychecks. The other half is paid by their employer. As a self-employed person, an independent contractor pays *both* halves of Social Security and Medicare taxes and so it is called something slightly different—self-employment tax.

This means an extra tax burden on independent contractors compared to employees. Many teenagers do not realize this extra tax burden when they start a micro business. This should not discourage you from starting a micro business—it just informs you of another responsibility you have to pay your taxes.

Worker Misclassification

The definitions of employee and independent contractor can be confusing. The IRS is not always very helpful when they say things like "whether people are employees or independent contractors depends on the facts in each case."[1] Sometimes employers, their teenage workers and the parents are all left confused.

Unfortunately, some adults take advantage of a teenager's lack of tax knowledge and try cheating them by reclassifying the teenager as an independent contractor when they should be classified as an employee.

> **True Story:** Last tax season, Todd's mother contacted me. Todd, a teenager, had been hired to

work in construction and thought he was an employee. Todd and his mother were confused and surprised to be given a 1099MISC form instead of a W-2. A 1099MISC form is given to independent contractors and showed that no taxes had been withheld or paid to the IRS. On the other hand, a W-2 is the form given to an *employee* to show the total income earned in a year and clearly shows how much tax was sent to the IRS on behalf of the employee. Imagine their surprise (and anger) when I explained that Todd was a self-employed business owner and would owe income tax as well as self-employment tax.

Was Todd an employee or an independent contractor? I discussed the facts of his work situation with his mother. He was hired by a business owner to do construction work. Todd and several other teenage boys used the business owner's tools, worked only for him all summer, and did what they were told (like employees). Todd should have been treated like an employee and had taxes withheld from his paycheck. I explained to his mother that the IRS has a procedure for complaints of worker misclassification. You can read about it at the **IRS.gov** website by searching "worker misclassification."

How could this misclassification of a worker happen? Todd's employer probably didn't want to do the extra paperwork involved with employees. Maybe he was trying to avoid paying employer taxes like Social Security and Medicare, unemployment insurance tax, or worker's compensation. Todd was paid with a check or in cash each week, but no pay stub showing his tax withholdings was ever given to him. This was a clue that something was wrong.

Learn a lesson from Todd and look at any paycheck you receive to see if Social Security (called FICA on a pay stub) and Medicare taxes have been withheld. If it is not clear, show your paycheck to your parents. Then ask your boss if you are classified as an employee or an independent contractor. Worker misclassification is widespread, and, unfortunately, teenagers are frequently victims. The IRS takes the issue of worker misclassification very seriously. If you feel you have been misclassified, the IRS is your friend and ally. Read the IRS website and Form SS-8 "Determination of Worker Status" at **IRS.gov** for more information on what you can do.

Important Points

- There are two general worker classifications: employee and independent contractor.
- Usually, micro business owners are independent contractors.
- Household employees do not pay self-employment tax.
- Independent contractors pay self-employment tax.
- Worker misclassification is very common, especially among teenage workers.

Chapter Seven
More Taxes:
State, Local, and Employer Taxes

In Chapter Five, I discussed federal income tax and self-employment tax, but there are several other types of taxes to consider including sales tax, state and local taxes, and employer taxes. In Chapter Eight, I will discuss sales tax. This chapter covers state, local, and employer taxes you may need to pay.

State and Local Income Tax

Most states and cities will tax your profit from a business regardless of your age, just like the Internal Revenue Service. Most states will let you file your taxes for your micro business on your state's personal tax return filed at the end of the year. Each state and locality has its own income tax forms, but they usually take the federal Schedule C (or the shorter C-EZ) as a record of business income.

> **Example:** In my state of Ohio, a teenage micro business owner files a tax return called an IT-1040, the form for individual taxpayers. The form takes total income from the federal Form 1040, and does not ask for business income to be shown separately. But many cities in Ohio frequently ask for a copy of the business form, Schedule C or C-EZ, to be attached to a city tax return.

A few states or towns will offer exemptions from tax if you are under age 18. Check with a local professional tax preparer to see if you might be exempt from state or local income tax because of your age.

> **True story:** Lucas lives in the city of Loveland, Ohio (funny name, but a nice place to live). Loveland does not tax small business income for taxpayers under the age of 18. Once Lucas turns 18, he will have to pay city income tax of 1% of his profit to the City of Loveland.

Employer Taxes

Federal income tax, self-employment tax, state and local income taxes...is your head spinning yet? It can be hard to keep it all straight (that's where a local accountant can help), and now I am throwing another type of tax at you: employer taxes. These are taxes that an employer pays on the wages he pays his employees. The most common employer taxes are Social Security and Medicare taxes.

Some states require employers to pay workers' compensation tax (in case a worker is injured on the job) and unemployment taxes (when a worker is laid off from his job). The taxes for workers' compensation and unemployment taxes vary by state, so talk to a local accountant about these taxes *before you hire an employee.*

In general, I discourage teenage micro business owners from hiring employees for several reasons:

- Micros are supposed to be easy to start and to end. If you have employees depending on you for their income, it is harder to close down the business.
- Micros are simple businesses, but employing workers is not simple. There are taxes to pay, forms to fill out, and deadlines to worry about.
- Micros should stay manageable so you can still have a life outside of your business. Managing people is one of the most difficult issues for any business owner. I recommend that teenagers focus on learning business skills now and wait until they are more experienced before hiring employees.

Chapter Nine offers an alternative to hiring employees—hiring independent contractors to do specific tasks. Independent contractors are workers that you can hire for a project or task such as web design or tax preparation. They are not treated as your employees. I recommend you consider hiring independent contractors to help in your micro business instead of employees.

All that being said, I will share some basic information on the taxes you will pay if you do hire employees.

Checklist for Hiring Employees (if you must)

- Visit the Department of Labor website for teenagers called YouthRules! at **YouthRules.dol.gov**. You will learn what jobs a teen employee can perform (or not perform) and what hours they can work.

- Get an Employer Identification Number (EIN) from the Internal Revenue Service (IRS). An EIN is like a social security number for businesses. They are offered for free by the IRS. To get your EIN go to **www.IRS.gov** and search for "EIN." You can fill in Form SS-4 on-line or print it out for mailing. Keep a copy for yourself. If you are in a hurry, you can apply by telephone (call the IRS at 1-800- 829-4933), fax, or on-line.

- Read IRS Publication 15 "Employers Tax Guide." It has a checklist of forms and dates that you will need to file. Publication 15A "Employer's Supplemental Tax Guide" has helpful information on worker classification and in-dependent contractor status. View the publications at the IRS website **www.IRS.gov**.

- Visit the **IRS.gov** website and search "Employment Taxes" for a list of taxes including Social Security tax, Medicare, and federal unemployment tax.

- Make an appointment with a local Certified Public Ac-countant (CPA) to discuss employer taxes and how much you can afford to pay an employee. A CPA can also give you the necessary forms you will need to col-lect from each worker and file with your state and local governments. They may help you find a bookkeeper or a payroll service to help you process your payroll.

- Check your budget and financial projections to be sure there will be enough money to pay the worker (including the taxes on that worker). A business owner might think that an employee will "pay for himself," by bringing in more business, but that is a risky assumption. Your CPA can help you make a budget and an estimate of how much it will cost to hire an employee.

- Agree on compensation arrangements with the worker. Know what the minimum wage requirements are for your state and local area. Start at the Department of Labor website, **www.DOL.gov** and search for "minimum wage laws."

- Collect Form W-4 from employees. It requests their legal name, address and tax identification number (usually their Social Security number). Get the form from the IRS website, **www.IRS.gov** and search for "Form W-4."

- Collect Form I-9 Employment Eligibility Verification Form from each employee. This is an immigration form from the department of Homeland Security to be sure you're not hiring illegal workers. Get the form at: **http://www.uscis.gov/files/form/i-9.pdf.**

As you can see, there is quite a bit of responsibility in hiring an employee. If you are not willing to read a lot, meet with a CPA, fill out forms, and plan for the extra expense and taxes of hiring employees, you should wait until you are ready. It is a big step to hire employees, but like everything else in running a micro business, you will learn a lot!

Example: Lucas had been running his lawn care micro business for three years when he needed to hire some help, especially during the busy grass-mowing season. He hired three hard-working, trustworthy friends and agreed on a fair amount to pay them. Then he met with me, his CPA, to go over the forms he needed to collect from each worker. We also discussed getting an EIN, what taxes Lucas would be paying, and the deadlines for filing forms and paying the tax. It was quite a responsibility for a 17-year-old guy, but Lucas was an experienced micro business owner and we both felt he could handle the extra responsibility and paperwork (with my help).

Social Security and Medicare Taxes

As an employer, you must withhold some of the money you pay to employees to pay payroll taxes, specifically Social Security and Medicare taxes. Then you, as the employer, must match the amount withheld from your business profits and send the total amount in to the United States federal government every quarter. The amount you must withhold from an employee equals 7.65% of their wages. You match that with another 7.65% and send in a total of 15.3% of all employees' wages to the IRS.

Example: Rich has three employees, and at the end of March (the end of the first quarter) he finds that he has paid his employees a total of $820 in wages. He withheld 7.65% of these wages ($62.73). Rich must match the $62.73 and send in a total of $125.46 to the IRS to cover his payroll taxes.

If your payroll taxes are less than $2,500 in a quarter, you can pay these taxes once a quarter. The IRS has a form (Form 941) that should be filled out and included with the tax payment.

It is very important for an employer to pay the payroll tax in full and on time. You must set aside money to pay these taxes. The IRS is not forgiving if you spent the money to pay your payroll tax on something else. Some small businesses open up a separate bank account to hold their payroll taxes, so that they do not spend the money on something else.

Many small businesses find that a payroll service can be very helpful. A payroll service can create paychecks with the proper withholding, fill in the IRS forms, and pay the taxes on time. A micro business owner could also use software such as QuickBooks to process their payroll. Other micro business owners look for a bookkeeper or an accountant to help them with payroll taxes.

The important thing to remember about payroll taxes is that they must be withheld from your employees' paychecks, paid on time, and done correctly. It is usually worth the expense to hire someone to do payroll processing for you, so you are sure it is done correctly.

Unemployment Taxes

If you hire employees, you may also have to pay federal unemployment tax (called FUTA). If you pay wages of $1,500 or more to employees in any calendar quarter you must pay federal unemployment taxes. Fifteen hundred dollars in a quarter would be a lot of wages for most teenage micro business owners. Note it is $1,500 in a quarter—three months—not a full year. Most teenage micro business owners fall below this threshold and often do not owe federal unemployment tax. See Instructions to Form 940 for details (**http://www.irs.gov/pub/irs-pdf/i940.pdf**)

The FUTA tax is a single flat rate of 6.2% on the first $7,000 of wages that you pay each employee. Once an employee's wages for the calendar year exceed $7,000, you have no more FUTA tax for that employee for the year.

States also charge a federal unemployment tax. Most employers pay both a federal and a state unemployment tax. State unemployment tax rates are based on your history of having to lay off a worker. Lower tax rates go to employers who have the lowest unemployment experience. Many states also limit the amount you must pay for each employee and have a maximum wage amount to which the tax applies.

For example, in Indiana, the state unemployment tax rate is 2.7% for new employers with a wage limit of $9,500. Wisconsin has rates that vary from 0-8.5% with a wage limit of $12,000.

Contact your state's department of taxation or employment for details. This website has general information about unemployment taxes by state: **http://www.toolkit.com/small_business_guide/sbg.asp x?nid=P07_1294.**

A local CPA can be extremely helpful if you have questions about unemployment taxes.

Workers' Compensation

What if one of your workers is hurt while working for you? Could you be responsible for their hospital bills? Yes, you could! Nearly every state has a system to help workers and their employers pay for work-related injuries called a workers' compensation system.

In most states, workers' compensation coverage is mandatory, but some states exempt very small employers from paying the workers' compensation tax. The most common exemption is for employers with fewer than three employees, but some states go up to five employees before they require paying the workers' compensation tax. This is good news for most teenage micro business owners, if they have fewer than five employees.

This website has general information about workers compensation taxes by state:
http://www.toolkit.com/small_business_guide/sbg.asp x?nid=P05_4403.

Employer Forms

As mentioned earlier, there are several forms to file and taxes to pay when you hire an employee. A local CPA can help you fill in the paperwork, but you should understand that it is your responsibility as the employer to file the correct forms on time. IRS Publication 15 "Employers Tax Guide" has a checklist of forms and dates that you will need to file. View it at the Internal Revenue Service (IRS) website **www.IRS.gov**.

You should give a Form W-4 to each employee to collect their information and federal income tax withholding. The W-4 is kept by you and not mailed into the IRS.

You, as the employer, will be responsible for paying federal employer taxes or payroll taxes (Social Security and Medicare) and filing quarterly statements with the IRS (called a Form 941). The form on the following page shows the first few lines of the Form 941. On lines 5 a, b and c, the employer calculates the total payroll taxes to be paid, including the portion withheld from the employees' paychecks and the employer matching portion. Your accountant, a payroll service, or accounting software can prepare these forms.

The IRS also has an electronic filing and payment system called Electronic Federal Tax Payment System (EFTPS). You can schedule a payment, and it will automatically be taken from your checking or savings account on the date you choose. Read about it at the IRS website **www.IRS.gov,** and search for "EFTPS."

Form 941 for 2010: Employer's QUARTERLY Federal Tax Return
(Rev. April 2010)   Department of the Treasury — Internal Revenue Service

951110
OMB No. 1545-0029

(EIN)
Employer identification number [ ] [ ] – [ ][ ][ ][ ][ ][ ]

Name (not your trade name)

Trade name (if any)

Address
Number   Street   Suite or room number

City   State   ZIP code

Report for this Quarter of 2010
(Check one.)

[ ] 1: January, February, March

[ ] 2: April, May, June

[ ] 3: July, August, September

[ ] 4: October, November, December

Read the separate instructions before you complete Form 941. Type or print within the boxes.

Part 1: Answer these questions for this quarter.

1 Number of employees who received wages, tips, or other compensation for the pay period
including: Mar. 12 (Quarter 1), June 12 (Quarter 2), Sept. 12 (Quarter 3), or Dec. 12 (Quarter 4)   1 [   ]

2 Wages, tips, and other compensation . . . .   2 [   ]

3 Income tax withheld from wages, tips, and other compensation . . . .   3 [   ]

4 If no wages, tips, and other compensation are subject to social security or Medicare tax   [ ] Check and go to line 6e.

	Column 1	Column 2
5a Taxable social security wages* .	[ ]	× .124 = [ ]
5b Taxable social security tips* . .	[ ]	× .124 = [ ]
5c Taxable Medicare wages & tips*	[ ]	× .029 = [ ]

*Report wages/tips for this quarter, including those paid to qualified new employees, on lines 5a–5c. The social security tax exemption on wages/tips will be figured on lines 6c and 6d and will reduce the tax on line 6e.

5d Add Column 2 line 5a, Column 2 line 5b, and Column 2 line 5c . . . .   5d [   ]

At the end of the year you will give a W-2 to each employee by January 31 and mail copies of the W-2 (and a summary of all W-2s called a W-3) to the IRS by February 28. See IRS Publication 15 for details.

22222   a Employee's social security number   OMB No. 1545-0008

b Employer identification number (EIN) | 1 Wages, tips, other compensation | 2 Federal income tax withheld

c Employer's name, address, and ZIP code | 3 Social security wages | 4 Social security tax withheld
| 5 Medicare wages and tips | 6 Medicare tax withheld
| 7 Social security tips | 8 Allocated tips

d Control number | 9 Advance EIC payment | 10 Dependent care benefits

e Employee's first name and initial   Last name   Suff. | 11 Nonqualified plans | 12a
| 13 Statutory employee / Retirement plan / Third-party sick pay | 12b
| 14 Other | 12c
| | 12d

f Employee's address and ZIP code

| 15 State | Employer's state ID number | 16 State wages, tips, etc. | 17 State income tax | 18 Local wages, tips, etc. | 19 Local income tax | 20 Locality name |

Form W-2 Wage and Tax Statement   **2010**   Department of the Treasury—Internal Revenue Service

Copy 1—For State, City, or Local Tax Department

A payroll service, accounting software, or an accountant can help you prepare these forms.

Tax forms can be ordered from the IRS at **www.IRS.gov** or by calling 1-800-TAX-FORM (800-829-3676). Accounting software such as QuickBooks can print off W-2s and Form 941s, but you must have the approved forms with red ink for easy reading by the IRS scanners. Forms are also for sale in office supply stores. There are also on-line filing services, such as **www.FileTaxes.com,** that typically charge about $5.00 or less per employee for preparing a W-2.

I hope you can see from this chapter that hiring employees and paying payroll tax is a huge responsibility that involves extra taxes and paperwork that must be filed on time and prepared correctly. I usually discourage teenage micro business owners from hiring employees. It is too much work, too expensive, and too time-consuming. If you need help, there are alternatives to hiring employees. In Chapter Nine, I share several options to hiring employees.

Important Points

- State and local cities may have income taxes that affect micro business owners.
- Avoid hiring employees if you can, but learn about employer taxes if you must.
- The most common employer taxes are Social Security and Medicare taxes.
- You must withhold payroll taxes and then match the amount withheld.
- All states require unemployment taxes (when a worker is laid off from his job).
- Some states require employers to pay workers' compensation tax in case a worker is injured on the job.
- The taxes for workers' compensation and unemployment taxes vary by state, so talk to a local accountant about these taxes *before you hire an employee.*
- Hiring employees and paying payroll tax is a huge responsibility that involves extra taxes and paperwork that must be filed on time and prepared correctly.
- An accountant, payroll service, or accounting software can help you process payroll and its taxes.

Chapter Eight
Sales Tax

Sales tax in the United States is a simple idea: the government asks sellers to add a bit of tax, typically 5-10%, to an item's price. The seller collects the tax and sends it to the government, usually a state or city office. Unfortunately, for the micro business owner, sales tax collections can become quite complicated. There are rules about what is taxed and what is tax-free. For example, most goods sold must have sales tax added, but some states exempt food and clothing from sales tax. Additionally, some services are taxed and some groups, such as churches, do not pay sales tax (in some states).

True Story: I attended a day-long class on sales tax and I left with a headache. It was so complex! I was there to help a micro business client who was selling dozens of low-priced items both locally and by mail in several states. She also sold to both nonprofit organizations that were exempt from paying sales tax and to individuals who must pay sales tax. It was important to know all of our local and state sales tax rules to be sure the correct amounts of tax were being collected.

You, as a micro owner, may find yourself in a situation where you need to understand sales tax, and this chapter will explain the basic rules common in every state.

How Sales Tax Works

When you sell a product, you add on sales tax at a rate determined by your state and local government, collect the tax from your customers and then send it to your state. You act as a tax collector for your state government. Most states tax the sale of products, but many states also tax some services like lawn care services and snow shoveling. If you provide a service in your micro business, consult with a local Certified Public Accountant (CPA) or call your state's sales tax department to determine if your service is a sales taxable business.

There are two ways to collect sales tax. You can add the tax on to your selling price or you can include the sales tax in your price. The advantage of adding on sales tax is that the customer clearly sees your price as separate from the sales tax, while the advantage of including sales tax in the price is that it is easier on the customer to pay you.

Example: I sold some books at a workshop. I typically sell the books for $10 each. Sales tax in the local area was 5%, making the sales tax $.50 for each book. It was easier for the audience to hand me $10 for a book and not have to find $.50 more to pay the sales tax. Instead, I paid the sales tax for the buyer, rather than add it to each book.

Later I calculated the sales tax I owed from the total books I sold and sent that amount into my state tax department. Here is how I calculated the sales tax:

Sale Price of Book = $10.00. Sales tax rate= 5%
Price of book alone = $10.00/(1.05) = $9.52
Sales Tax = $10.00 - $9.52 = $.48 per book

For every $10 book I sold, $9.52 was my income and $0.48 was sales tax I owed to the state.

State Requirements

Most states have a website that explains their sales tax rules. Most states only tax retail sales. Retail sales are the sale to the final customer. Wholesale sales are usually not subject to sales tax. Wholesale sales are usually large quantity sales sold to someone other than the final consumer such as to a business or manufacturer.

Example: Julie makes candy. When she sells to consumers, she must add sales tax because they are retail sales to the final customer. Occasionally, she sells a large number of boxes of candy to a gift store, Mandy's Gifts. These are wholesale sales and Julie does not collect sales tax on this wholesale sale. When Mandy sells the candy in her gift store, she charges sales tax to her customers.

Some states tax only materials you sell to customers, such as a lawn service selling mulch, while some charge sales tax on labor costs also.

True Story: Lucas runs a micro business mowing lawns. The state of Ohio recently passed a law that lawn services are a sales-taxable transaction. That means that Lucas had to add on sales tax to his price for mowing a lawn.

This website will help you determine what your state and local laws are concerning sales tax: **www.taxadmin.org/fta/link/.**

For example, this is the sales tax law in Virginia:

A seller is subject to the sales tax imposed on gross receipts from retail sales. "Retail sales" means sales made for any purpose other than for resale. The tax may also apply to the furnishing of transient accommodations and the lease or rental of personal property.

The seller collects the tax from the customer on each sale. The tax must be separately stated and added to the sales price or charge. The general sales tax rate is 5% (4% state tax and 1% local tax).[2]

Consult With a Local CPA

Sales tax rules are complex and vary from state to state. Consult your state's sales tax office or a local accountant. A local accountant, familiar with your county, city, and state tax laws, can be very helpful in knowing when sales tax applies to your micro business.

Do not trust local business owners or on-line small business forums to give you accurate information. They may be honest and helpful, but they may be wrong, because states change their sales tax laws quite frequently. Go to the source—your state's sales tax department or a local accountant—for accurate information.

True Story: Looking at the sales tax law in my state more closely, I, as Lucas' CPA, learned that lawn care services were sales taxable if annual sales were $5,000 or more. Since Lucas earned only $4,000, he did not have to collect sales tax from his customers.

Obtain a Vendor's License

Most states require businesses to apply for a vendor's license if they make sales-taxable transactions. Sometimes the state calls it a business tax registration or a sales tax permit. This website, **www.taxadmin.org/fta/link/,** will lead you to the registration information for your state.

Many states have a variety of vendor's licenses. Many require special licenses if you are operating specific businesses or selling specific goods such as tobacco, alcohol, gasoline, or fireworks. These rules should not apply to most teenage micro business owners.

Many states are now accepting on-line applications for vendor's licenses. Your state will send you the proper sales tax information and forms when you apply for a vendor's license or register your business.

What Is Needed to Apply?

The information needed to apply for a vendor's license will vary by state, but most require your name, business name, address, a social security number, and an NAICS code.

Here is a part of Ohio's application for a vendor's license:

The North American Industry Classification System (NAICS) is used by the United States federal government to collect statistics about businesses. You can search for a

NAICS code that matches your micro business here: http://www.naics.com/search.htm.

Example: The NAICS code for my accounting business is 541211 Offices of Certified Public Accountants. My other business, writing books, has an NAICS code of 71150 Artists, Writers, and Performers.

Some parts of a vendor's license application may be confusing to you. Do not guess at your answers. Instead, ask a local accountant or call your state sales tax office. I have done this several times and find the state employees can be very helpful. They have saved me hours of time trying to find an answer on the internet.

Call Your State's Sales Tax Office
Sometimes a state's sales tax laws can be difficult to understand, so do not be afraid to call your state's sales tax office. Rehearse what you will ask before calling and say something like, "I'm starting a new business selling _____. Will I need to collect sales tax?" Then ask for information to be mailed (or e-mailed) to you. Do not hang up without getting confirmation that something will be sent to you. Get it in writing, especially if they say your business is not subject to sales tax.

True Story: Brent started a business helping homeowners find energy leaks in their home. He used an infrared camera to see where heat was escaping. This was a new type of business, so he called his state's sales tax department and was told that his business did *not* have to collect sales tax.

I doubted this statement by the state employee because my state loves to tax everything. "Did you get that in writing?" I asked Brent. He had not. Nor had he gotten the employee's name or a record of what date he made the call. These records would help prove that Brent attempted to gain accurate information if the income was indeed sales taxable.

Out-of-State Sales

If you sell products to a customer out of state, you do *not* have to collect or pay sales tax on that sale. Why not? It has to do with a complicated legal term called "nexus." Nexus means a connection or link or, in the case of sales tax rules, it means having a physical presence in a state. If you do not have a physical presence in a state, like an office or a salesperson, then you do not have nexus in that state. No nexus, then no sales tax. The concept goes way back into American history and our Constitution where states were not allowed to tax an out-of-state business.

> **Example:** Tia sells a book she wrote via her website. She must charge sales tax to customers in her state, but not to customers in other states. Tia knows what state her customers live in from their order form and she adds sales tax for customers in her state.

Like everything having to do with sales tax, nexus rules vary by state also. (You may be starting to see why I left my day-long seminar on sales tax with a headache!) If you do business in a state where you have a "physical presence," even if only for a few days, you generally have to collect sales tax from customers in that state.

True Story: I was invited to sell my books at a home-school convention in Virginia. Because I *physically* went to Virginia for the convention, I had nexus in that state. I collected Virginia sales tax on all my book sales for the three-day convention. After I got home, I added up my sales, filled out a Virginia sales tax form, and mailed them a check. If I had stayed in Ohio and sold books to customers in Virginia by mail (but not physically entered the state to conduct business), I would *not* have had to collect or pay sales tax on those sales.

Some states also require out-of-state vendors to obtain a temporary vendor's license. I had to do that when I traveled to Pennsylvania to sell my books at a convention there. The form was easy to fill in on-line, but it needed to be filed before I conducted sales in Pennsylvania. It is important to know the sales tax laws of a state before you begin selling while in that state.

Internet Based Sales

Most internet-based micro businesses can sell goods without having to charge or collect sales tax. It is because of the concept of nexus again. Most of your sales might be from out-of-state customers. You will have to know where a customer lives and then charge only your in-state customers sales tax. Internet shopping carts can be a great help with calculating sales tax.

Many authors use print-on-demand services, electronic shopping cart programs, or digital information product service providers such as Clickbank, to sell and deliver their books and ebooks. Many times these services will collect sales tax from customers and pay the proper taxing authorities. This makes collecting and paying sales tax invisible to the author, who merely collects a royalty check.

Example: Several of my books are sold via **CreateSpace.com** (a print on demand publisher), as a print book and via **Clickbank.com** as an ebook. Both CreateSpace.com and Clickbank.com collect the proper sales tax from each customer and pay each state as needed. It is completely invisible to me. I love these services and the convenience they offer!

In addition, some states do not apply sales tax to electronic materials. They tax only tangible personal property—things you can touch and feel.

Example: Cindy sells an ebook (an electronic book) on her website, but her state does not charge sales tax on electronic materials. Her state only charges sales tax on tangible personal property. She does not need to collect information from her customers on where they live or charge any of her customers sales tax. Check to see if your state taxes the sale of electronic materials.

The rules on internet sales are changing very quickly as more states try to collect sales tax revenues. Many states are trying to tax internet sales and there have been several recent court cases from Amazon.com and other large internet-based companies over paying sales tax. It is important to have a business adviser such as a local CPA who can inform you when laws affecting internet-based businesses change.

Paying the Sales Tax

For most micro businesses, sales tax will need to be paid only annually or quarterly, but that can vary depending on your state law and the amount of sales you make. Very large retailers must pay sales tax monthly. For example, in New York State you file a sales tax return only once a year if you owe $3,000 or less in sales tax for the year. The form and tax payment are due March 30.

Mark your calendar with the sales tax due date for your state and send it in on-time or early. If you are late, you will probably be charged a fine.

Texas has a short sales tax form that some small businesses can use as shown below.

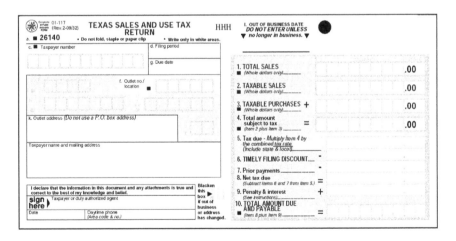

If the form your state uses to pay your sales tax confuses you, find a local CPA that can help explain and fill in the form for you. After a few times, you might be able to prepare the form yourself. Many of my teenage micro owners prepare their own sales tax forms after I show them how.

Important Points

- Sales tax collections can become quite complicated.
- It is important to understand sales tax, especially in your state.
- Consult with a local CPA or your state sales tax department to receive accurate information.
- Most states only tax retail sales, not wholesale sales to another business.
- Most states require business owners to apply for a vendor's license if they make sales-taxable transactions.
- Understand out-of-state sales tax and when you need to collect sales tax from out-of-state customers.
- If you have a "physical presence," even if only for a few days, you generally have to collect sales tax from customers in that state.
- The rules on internet sales are changing very quickly.
- Pay your taxes on time.

Chapter Nine
Hiring Help: Employees and Independent Contractors

What should a micro business owner do if he or she needs help? You can hire employees who will do whatever you tell them (hopefully), hire independent contractors who will do a specific job, or send customers to another micro business.

In general, I discourage teenage micro business owners form hiring employees for several reasons. Hiring employees involves:

- Paperwork
- Understanding legal requirements
- Paying taxes
- Filing tax forms
- Training employees
- Overseeing employees as they work

- Dealing with personnel issues such as poor work habits, tardiness, unavailability, theft ,and insubordination (when your employees do not respect you as their boss)

Alternatives to Hiring Employees

Rather than hiring employees, I recommend finding another person that you can hire as an independent contractor to do a specific project. In writing this book, I hired several independent contractors:

- A graphic designer to do the book cover
- An editor to read over the book and correct my mistakes
- A book designer to help with initial layout of the pages
- A virtual assistant to help set up the shopping cart on my website

None of these people are my employees; they were hired for a specific task and that is all. I paid an agreed-upon price to do the task. They are all micro business owners and some of them are teenagers!

If you are overloaded with work, another option instead of hiring employees, is to encourage another teenager to take over some of your workload and start their own micro business. No one can do it all by himself and you will hurt yourself by trying. If there is too much business for you to do alone, both you and your customers will suffer. Instead, tell a friend about my website and books, and encourage them to start their own business. Help them out by giving them a few of your clients, so your life is more manageable.

Two Categories of Workers

A paid worker falls into one of two categories:
- an employee
- an independent contractor

Employee
According to the United States Internal Revenue Service (IRS), anyone who performs services for you is your employee *if you can control what will be done and how it will be done.* You, as the boss, have the right to control the details of how the services are performed.

If a worker is an employee you must give him or her a W-2 and file copies with the Internal Revenue Service. In addition, federal income tax, Social Security, and Medicare taxes must be withheld and paid quarterly. See IRS Publication 15 at **www.IRS.gov** and Chapter Seven of this book for details on the proper IRS forms for employees.

Independent Contractor
On the other hand, a worker is an independent contractor if you—the person for whom the services are performed—has the right to control only the *result* of the work and not how the work is performed. In other words, the independent contractor performs a job or a project and doesn't need to be told how to do the task.

If the worker is an *independent contractor* the business

owner must give each worker making more than $600 in a calendar year a Form 1099MISC and file copies with the IRS. Federal income tax, Social Security, and Medicare taxes are not withheld nor paid. The independent contractor is responsible for reporting income on Schedule C of the Form 1040 and paying self-employment tax. See the IRS Publication 15A at **www.IRS.gov** and the section of this chapter titled "Forms For Independent Contractors" for details.

Worker Classification: A Critical Issue

The issue of worker status has gotten a lot of attention lately as the Internal Revenue Service scrutinizes under-reporting of income by independent contractors and mis-classification by the businesses that hire them. It is very important that micro business owners become familiar with employment regulations and taxes before hiring a worker.

A micro business can hire a worker as an employee or as an independent contractor. The difference can be confusing, but important. The difference depends on how much control the business owner has over the worker. The facts of the situation determine worker status, not the owner's preference. Many micro business owners do not want to deal with the paperwork of withholding and paying employment taxes, creating W-2s, etc. It is easier to deal with a contractor than an employee. However, the IRS reminds us that the facts and circumstances of the relationship determine worker status, not the owner's preference.

How To Determine Worker Status

The IRS uses three factors to determine worker classification:
* Behavioral Control
* Financial Control
* Type of Relationship

Behavioral Control covers whether the business has a right to direct or control how the work is done. This could be through giving instructions or training. In other words, an independent contractor needs no instructions or training to do their job; they already know how to do their job.

Example: When I hired a graphic designer to create some book covers for me, I looked for someone with a graphic design background. I hired Dave Huff, an experienced designer, who had all the tools (software) he needed. He quoted me a price to do three book covers. We discussed what I wanted for my covers, but I did not tell him how to do his job, what software to use or how many hours he should spend. I exercised no behavioral control since Dave was an independent contractor.

Financial Control covers whether the business has a right to direct or control the financial aspects of the worker's job. This includes:

* The extent to which the worker has business expenses.
* The extent of the worker's investment in the facilities used in performing services.
* The extent to which the worker makes his or her

services available to the relevant market.
- How the business pays the worker.
- The extent to which the worker can realize a profit or incur a loss. [3]

Contractors should be paid by the job, not by the hour. Employees are paid by the hour, but contractors are paid for doing a job. I recommend that micro business owners negotiate a payment for a job, not an hourly rate, with contractors.

Type of Relationship covers how the parties perceive their relationship. This includes:

- Written contracts describing the relationship the parties intend to create.
- The extent to which the worker is available to perform services for other, similar businesses.
- Whether the business provides the worker with employee-type benefits, such as insurance, a pension plan, vacation pay, or sick pay.
- The permanency of the relationship.
- The extent to which services performed by the worker are a key aspect of the regular business of the company. [4]

Many independent contractors hired by micro business owners also offer their services to the general public as web designers, graphic designers, etc. I strongly recommend you have a signed agreement with every contractor that you hire. It should clearly state that they are hired as independent contractors, not employees. If applicable, state the length of the agreement, so it is not assumed to be a permanent arrangement.

The IRS has a brochure, *Independent Contractor or Employee* (Publication 1779), to help organizations determine worker status at **www.IRS.gov.**

Can't Decide? Let the IRS Help

The IRS can make a worker classification for you if you desire. Fill in Form SS-8 from the IRS website **www.IRS.gov,** and they will make a determination for you. This service is usually used by disgruntled workers who thought they should be classified as employees. These workers request the IRS to investigate in hopes of getting employee benefits such as insurance or to avoid paying self-employment tax.

I suggest you consider this option carefully, since you will have to live with the IRS's decision. If they determine you have employees, you will have to file the proper paperwork mentioned in the following section and pay employment taxes. Your business may owe back taxes from prior years. You may also be liable to your state for unemployment taxes for the years that the workers were misclassified.

Forms for Independent Contractors

Give a Form W-9 to each independent contractor to collect their legal name and social security number. If they operate under a business name, they may provide you with an EIN number (Employer Identification Number), instead of a social security number. Use the independent contractor's

EIN on the end-of-year 1099MISC form. The W-9 is kept by you and not mailed to the IRS.

Form **W-9** (Rev. October 2007) Department of the Treasury Internal Revenue Service	**Request for Taxpayer Identification Number and Certification**	Give form to the requester. Do not send to the IRS.

Name (as shown on your income tax return)

Business name, if different from above

Check appropriate box: ☐ Individual/Sole proprietor ☐ Corporation ☐ Partnership
☐ Limited liability company. Enter the tax classification (D=disregarded entity, C=corporation, P=partnership) ▶ _____
☐ Other (see instructions) ▶

☐ Exempt payee

Address (number, street, and apt. or suite no.)   Requester's name and address (optional)

City, state, and ZIP code

List account number(s) here (optional)

Part I   Taxpayer Identification Number (TIN)

Enter your TIN in the appropriate box. The TIN provided must match the name given on Line 1 to avoid backup withholding. For individuals, this is your social security number (SSN). However, for a resident alien, sole proprietor, or disregarded entity, see the Part I instructions on page 3. For other entities, it is your employer identification number (EIN). If you do not have a number, see How to get a TIN on page 3.

Note. If the account is in more than one name, see the chart on page 4 for guidelines on whose number to enter.

Social security number | | | |
or
Employer identification number

At the end of the year, give each contractor that has earned over $600 a 1099MISC form. Put the total amount of compensation paid during the year in Box 7 (Nonemployee compensation).

PAYER'S name, street address, city, state, ZIP code, and telephone no.	1 Rents $	OMB No. 1545-0115 **2011** Form 1099-MISC	**Miscellaneous Income**
	2 Royalties $		
	3 Other income $	4 Federal income tax withheld $	Copy 1 **For State Tax Department**
PAYER'S federal identification number	RECIPIENT'S identification number	5 Fishing boat proceeds $	6 Medical and health care payments $	
RECIPIENT'S name		7 Nonemployee compensation $	8 Substitute payments in lieu of dividends or interest $	
Street address (including apt. no.)		9 Payer made direct sales of $5,000 or more of consumer products to a buyer (recipient) for resale ▶ ☐	10 Crop insurance proceeds $	
City, state, and ZIP code		11	12	
Account number (see instructions)		13 Excess golden parachute payments $	14 Gross proceeds paid to an attorney $	
15a Section 409A deferrals $	15b Section 409A income $	16 State tax withheld $	17 State/Payer's state no.	18 State income $

Form **1099-MISC**   Department of the Treasury - Internal Revenue Service

1099MISC forms must be given to the independent contractor no later than January 31. Send a copy to the IRS along with Form 1096 by February 28. You have until March 31 to file 1099MISC and Form 1096 if you file them electronically. Retain a copy for your records.

Tax forms can be ordered from the IRS at **www.IRS.gov** or by calling 1-800-TAX-FORM (800-829-3676). Forms are also for sale in office supply stores. Accounting software, such as QuickBooks, can print off 1099MISC forms, but you must have the approved forms with red ink for easy reading by the IRS scanners. There are also on-line filing services, such as **www.FileTaxes.com**, that typically charge under $5.00 per worker.

Federal income tax, Social Security, and Medicare taxes are *not* withheld for independent contractors. The independent contractor is responsible for reporting income on Schedule C of the Form 1040 and paying self-employment tax. More information can be found in the IRS's Publication 15A "Employers Supplemental Tax Guide."

Forms for employees (W-4, W-2, and Form 941) are discussed in Chapter Seven.

Important Points

- If your micro business needs help, you can hire employees, hire an independent contractor, or send customers to another micro business.
- There are two types of workers: employees and independent contractors.
- Hiring employees involves paperwork, legal requirements, and taxes.
- The IRS has a criteria to determine independent contractor status.
- There are special IRS forms for employees and independent contractors.

Chapter Ten
Working With an Accountant

Micro business owners might delay working with an accountant until they think they can afford it, but this can be harmful to a new business. Knowledge that is too little or too late can be very expensive.

Set aside some of your first dollars of profit toward getting good business advice. Better yet, meet with an accountant *before* you start your business. They could help you avoid costly mistakes and unnecessary expenses.

True Story: One client I met with had started a service micro business doing energy evaluations of homes and businesses using an infrared camera. He thought that he needed a vendor's license from the state government, so he applied to be a vendor and paid a $25 fee. He did not need a vendor's license because he wasn't selling any products or collecting sales tax. After he ignored filing the sales tax forms, he received a tax bill for over $1,000! "How can this be?" he thought. After several calls to the State Department of Taxation, he got the tax bill removed. He would have been smarter, and a little richer, to have asked a Certified Public Accountant (CPA) if he needed to apply for a vendor's license.

What a CPA Can Do For You

Most small business owners only use their accountants to prepare their tax returns. Taxes are complicated and professional help is often needed, but a good CPA can help your business in many ways besides just tax preparation:

- Calculate estimated taxes which are payments made to the IRS and your state during the year
- Assist with accurate record keeping
- Explain the pros and cons of forming a partnership or becoming a corporation
- Help you take all the deductions to which you are entitled
- Determine eligibility for the business use of the home deduction
- Calculate depreciation of business equipment as a tax deduction
- Assist you in preparing payroll taxes and filing payroll reports

No one is an expert at everything, so I encourage you to focus on what you do best—running your business—and leave tax and accounting matters to those who know them best. To keep accounting fees down, you can hire a bookkeeper at a lower rate than a CPA, or do all the record keeping yourself and only meet with your accountant when needed.

How Much Do CPAs Charge?

Naturally CPA fees vary depending on your location and their experiences. A typical rate for a one-hour consultation with a small business CPA might cost you $100 to $150. Many CPAs will meet with a new business owner for 30 to 60 minutes for no charge.

A recent survey (December, 2009) by the National Society of Accountants[5] found that the tax preparation fees for a sole proprietorship business tax form (Schedule C) was $212. These fees do not include the tax return for an individual which averaged $229 for a Form 1040 with itemized deductions (Schedule A) and a state return. The survey found that tax preparation fees vary by region and size of the firm.

Get a clear understanding of what your future accounting fees might be. Many accountants charge a set monthly fee or will work on a project basis. You should be able to accurately budget what the accounting and tax preparation fees will cost your business. If your accountant is vague about fees, you may need to work with someone that can be specific about their fees so that you can plan for the expense.

Seek out an accountant that has the ability to teach you the financial side of your business. You should feel comfortable with him or her and be free to ask questions. If you leave a meeting with your accountant feeling confused, you need to find another accountant. To find a helpful professional, ask other small business owners in your area for their accountant's contact information or call your state CPA society. Find a listing at **www.taxsites.com/cpa-societies.htm.**

Questions to Ask an Accountant

The relationship between a micro business owner and accountant is very important. As a new business owner, you have a lot to learn, so seek out an accountant with the heart of a teacher. Interview several accountants, looking for someone that you understand. If you leave an interview more confused than you entered, keep looking. You should leave the meeting saying, "I learned a lot."

Interview a potential accountant and ask some questions:

- Tell me about your small business clients. Are they similar in size and industry? Any teenage clients?
- Could you share two or three names as referrals?
- How much do you charge?
- How often am I billed?
- What is included in your services?
- What is *not* included?

- How often will we meet? Where?
- What do I need to bring to our meetings?
- Why is bookkeeping important?
- Explain the reports that I will receive from you.

A good accountant will explain difficult subjects in a clear, understandable way. Use a few test questions to see if your accountant communicates well.

- What is depreciation? Why can't I deduct the cost of equipment in the year that I purchased it? (You can, and the accountant should explain a section 179 deduction.)

- What are the advantages of being a Limited Liability Company? What does limited liability mean? When should I consider forming an LLC?

- What are common deductions that micro business owners miss?

CPAs Speak IRS-ese

Most micro business owners know that they should consult with an accountant to help run their business better, but their real motivation to hiring a CPA is fear of the Internal Revenue Service (IRS). A CPA is qualified to represent taxpayers before the IRS if ever there is a question or problem with their tax returns. The CPA acts as an interpreter between the business owner and the government. This is a huge source of relief to many business owners who want nothing to do with the IRS. CPAs are trained to talk the talk that the IRS speaks and understand tax code better than a business owner. The CPA is on the taxpayer's side and it certainly helps to have someone in your corner if needed.

A True Story About an IRS Audit

A friend of mine got a letter from the IRS auditing their tax return from three years prior. She called me a day late, meaning she and her husband had already met with the IRS alone. They went thinking, "We're honest people; we have nothing to hide." Their integrity and honesty were not in question, their tax return was the issue. They were good, upright people, but they did not understand taxes, accounting, or the IRS.

I gave them the name of an experienced CPA and then went along when she went to talk to the IRS on their behalf. Here is what I learned and observed:

1. Never visit the IRS alone. *Always* hire a CPA to represent you. CPAs speak the IRS's language. They understand the tax laws and are not as emotionally involved as you, the taxpayer.

2. Let the CPA go it alone. You, as the taxpayer, do not have to go along to meet with the IRS. My friends felt their integrity was being challenged by the questions the IRS examiner asked, but the CPA representing them understood it was all just part of the process. She was calm and professional, while my friends would have been an emotional wreck.

3. Keep excellent records. Fortunately, my friend kept receipts for her business expenses from three years

ago. Some were pretty faded, but she had them. This helped tremendously. Keep deposit slips, bank statements, canceled checks, etc. Most banking is electronic these days, but the IRS still runs on paper.

4. Understand that the process is boring and tedious. Most of our three-hour visit was spent in watching the IRS examiner re-add the totals that the CPA (and taxpayer) had already added.

5. If you run a business, get a CPA to examine your tax return. You may want to prepare it yourself to save money, but ask a CPA to review it. A lot of problems could have been avoided if my friend had hired me for an hour of time to go over her tax return. She had put numbers on the wrong lines on her tax return and the IRS got suspicious.

I may sound a little self-serving since I am a CPA, but please get help with taxes and accounting when you start a business. Calling in help after the IRS contacts you is expensive, time consuming, and emotionally draining.

Important Points

- Get good business advice before starting a micro business.

- Focus on running your micro business and leave tax and accounting matters to your CPA.

- Seek out an accountant who can teach you the financial side of your business.

- Interview several accountants and look for someone that you can understand.

- A CPA is an interpreter between the business owner and the IRS.

Footnotes

1 http://www.irs.gov/businesses/small/article/0,,id=179115,00.html

2 http://www.tax.virginia.gov/site.cfm?alias=salesusetax

3 From the IRS's Topic 762 - Independent Contractor vs. Employee

4 From the IRS's Topic 762 - Independent Contractor vs. Employee

5 http://www.webcpa.com/news/-52744-1.html?st=RSS

About the Author

Carol Topp, CPA, owner of **www.CarolToppCPA.com** and **MicroBusinessForTeens.com,** helps people, especially teenagers, start their own small businesses.

Carol was born and raised in Racine, Wisconsin and graduated from Purdue University with a degree in engineering. She worked ten years for the US Navy as a cost analyst before staying home with her two daughters. While being a stay-at-home mom, Carol took accounting classes via distance learning. In 2000, Carol received her CPA license and opened her own practice.

She is a member of the Ohio Society of CPAs, the National Association of Tax Professionals, and the Society of Nonprofit Organizations. Carol has presented numerous workshops on money management, business start up, taxes, budgeting, and homeschooling to various community, church, and homeschool groups.

She has authored several books including:
- *Homeschool Co-ops: How to Start Them, Run Them and Not Burn Out*
- *Information in a Nutshell: Business Tips and Taxes for Writers*
- *Teens and Taxes: A Guide for Parents and Teenagers*

And several magazine articles in:
- *The Old Schoolhouse*
- *Home Education*
- *Homeschool Enrichment*
- National Association of Tax Professionals *TaxPro*
- *Nonprofit World*

Carol lives in Cincinnati, Ohio with her husband and two daughters where she runs her micro business from her home.

If you enjoyed *Money and Taxes in a Micro Business,* look for other books in the Micro Business for Teens series.

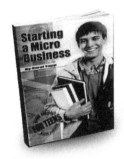

Starting a Micro Business covers the characteristics of a micro business, ideas, creating a business plan, starting with no debt, and staying motivated.

Running a Micro Business covers record keeping, inventory, selling products, time management, marketing, and customer service.

Micro Business for Teens Workbook is designed for individual or group study. Put into practice what you read in *Starting a Micro Business* and *Running a Micro Business.*

Also available are audios, webinars, and video instruction on starting and running a micro business.

Available at **MicroBusinessForTeens.com**